ALPHA-PHONICS

A Primer for Beginning Readers

Reading maketh a full man . . . and writing an exact man.

FRANCIS BACON

ALPHA-PHONICS

A Primer for Beginning Readers

by

Samuel L. Blumenfeld

THE PARADIGM COMPANY

Boise, Idaho

For information:
The Paradigm Co., Inc.

Email: alphaphonics@hotmail.com

Websites: www.alphaphonics.com

Manufactured in the United States of America

Fortieth Printing, September 2014

Library of Congress Cataloging in Publication Data

      Blumenfeld, Samuel L
      Alpha-Phonics.

      1. Reading (Elementary) 1. Title.
      LB1573.B5S8   1983   372.4'1   82 - 12873
      ISBN 978-1979228473

Books by Samuel L Blumenfeld:

How To Start Your Own Private School -
      And Why You Need One

The New Illiterates

How To Tutor

The Retreat From Motherhood

Is Public Education Necessary?

ALPHA-PHONICS: A Primer For Beginning Readers
(See back page for ordering information)

CONTENTS

PREFACE

ALPHA-PHONICS was created to provide teachers, tutors and parents with a sensible, logical, easy-to-use tool for teaching reading. It is an intensive phonics instruction program based on the author's many years of research and experience in the reading instruction field. It answers the need for a practical instruction book that anyone who wants to teach reading can learn to use with a minimum of training.

This program can be used to teach reading to beginners of all ages, older students in need of remediation and retraining, functional illiterates, dyslexics, special-needs students, the learning disabled, and non-English speakers who wish to learn to read English and improve their pronunciation.

It can also be used as a supplement to any other reading program being used in the classroom. Its systematic approach to teaching basic phonetic skills makes it particularly valuable to programs that lack such instruction.

The book's step by-step lessons in large, eye-pleasing calligraphy make it suitable for both direct one-on-one tutoring and regular classroom use. Parents who wish to teach their children to read at home will find the book particularly useful, since it is written in normal, every day English and is free of the professional jargon characteristic of so many reading instruction books.

All of the lesson pages were carefully designed to eliminate distraction and to focus the pupils full attention on the work at hand. The Teacher's Manual, in the back of the book, provides teachers and tutors with the necessary instructional information for each lesson. The program, as a whole, is flexible enough so that any teacher or tutor can adapt it to his or her own teaching style or situation.

If you have never taught reading before in this sensible, systematic way, you will be pleasantly surprised by the results.

—— Samuel L Blumenfeld

1

Aa Bb Cc Dd
Ee Ff Gg Hh
Ii Jj Kk Ll Mm
Nn Oo Pp Qq
Rr Ss Tt Uu Vv
Ww Xx Yy Zz

ALPHA-PHONICS: A Primer for Beginning Readers

Hand lettered by Marc Vachon

ă		
a	m	am
a	n	an
a	s	as
a	t	at
a	x	ax

NOTICE:

Parent/Teacher:

Your <u>complete</u> set of INSTRUCTIONS for EVERY lesson begins on page 131 (In back of book)

S	am	Sam
m	an	man
h	as	has
s	at	sat
t	ax	tax

S s

am   an   as   at   ax
Sam   man   has   hat   tax

Sam sat.
Sam has an ax.

Lesson 4

a	d		ad
d	ad		dad
w	ax		wax
D	an		Dan

Dan sat.
Dad has wax.

Dd

ad	am	an	as	at	ax
had	ham	man	has	hat	tax
dad	dam	Dan	[was]	sat	wax
sad	Sam	tan		mat	Max
Tad					
mad					

ad	dad	had	mad	sad
am	dam	ham	man	sat
an	Dan	has	Max	Sam
as		hat		
at				
ax				
	Tad		[was]	
	tan		wax	
	tax			

Mm   Hh   Tt

Dan has an ax.
Dan has ham.
Sam sat.
Has dad an ax?
Dad has wax.
Dad was sad.
Max was mad.
Tad was tan.
Dan has ham.
Sam was mad.
Was Dan mad?

an   d   and
                   hand
                   sand
l   and   land

Dan and dad had land and sand.

Dan and Sam.
Max and Tad.
Tax and wax.
Land and sand.

Ll   Aa

Ll

Al	Al
	Hal
	Sal

Bb

b	ad	bad
b	an	ban
b	and	band
b	at	bat

Cc

c	ab	cab
c	ad	cad
c	al	Cal
c	at	cat
c	an	can

Gg

g	ab		gab
g	ad		gad
g	ag		gag
g	al		gal
g	as		gas

Jj	Ff	Ll	Nn
jam	fad	lab	nab
Jan	fan	lag	nag
jab	fat	lad	Nat
	Fab		

Pp	Tt	Rr
pad	tab	rag
pal	Tab	ram
Pam	Tad	ran
pat	tag	rap
	tan	
	tap	
	tax	

Vv	Ww	Yy	Zz
Val	wag	yam	zag
van	wax	yap	
vat	was		

ad	Al	ag	ab
bad	Cal	bag	cab
cad	gal	gag	dab
dad	Hal	hag	Fab
fad	pal	lag	gab
had	Sal	nag	jab
lad	Val	rag	lab
mad		sag	nab
pad		tag	tab
sad		wag	
Tad			

am	an	ap	as
dam	ban	cap	gas
ham	can	lap	has
jam	Dan	map	was
Pam	fan	nap	
ram	Jan	rap	
Sam	man	sap	
yam	pan	tap	
	ran	yap	
	tan		
	van		

at	ax	az	and
bat	lax	Yaz	band
cat	Max	jazz	hand
fat	tax		land
hat	wax		sand
mat			
Nat			
pat			
rat			
sat			
vat			

$\boxed{\text{ck}}$

ack	Mack	tack
back	pack	yack
hack	rack	Zack
Jack	sack	$\boxed{\text{qu}}$
lack		quack

Lesson 12

a

a cat	a pal
a hat	a bag
a bat	a rag
a cap	a cab
a pan	a map

Al can bat.
Sal was fat.
Jack has a sack.
Pam has a fat cat.
Val has jam.
Jan has a cap.
Cal has a hat.
Yaz can bat.
Mack has a jazz band.
Yaz can yack.
Jack has a pack-sack.
Can Yaz bat?

ab	bab	cab	dab
ac	bac	cac	dac
ack	back	cack	dack
ad	bad	cad	dad
af	baf	caf	daf
ag	bag	cag	dag
al	bal	cal	dal
am	bam	cam	dam
an	ban	can	dan
ap	bap	cap	dap
as	bas	cas	das
at	bat	cat	dat
av	bav	cav	dav
ax	bax	cax	dax
az	baz	caz	daz

fab	gab	hab	jab
fam	gac	hac	jac
fat	gack	hack	Jack
fad	gad	had	jad
faf	gaf	haf	jaf
fav	gag	hag	jag
fal	gal	hal	jal
fam	gam	ham	jam
fan	gan	han	jan
fap	gap	hap	jap
fas	gas	has	jas
fat	gat	hat	jat
fav	gav	hav	jav
fax	gax	hax	jax
faz	gaz	haz	jaz

kab	lab	mab	nab
kac	lac	mac	nac
kack	lack	mack	nack
kad	lad	mad	nad
kaf	laf	maf	naf
kag	lag	mag	nag
kal	lal	mal	nal
kam	lam	mam	nam
kan	lan	man	nan
kap	lap	map	nap
kas	las	mas	nas
kat	lat	mat	nat
kav	lav	mav	nav
kax	lax	max	nax
kaz	laz	maz	naz

pab	quab	rab	sab
pac	quac	rac	sac
pack	quack	rack	sack
pad	quax	rad	sad
paf	quaf	raf	saf
pag	quag	rag	sag
pal	quap	ral	sal
pam	quaz	ram	sam
pan	quack	ran	san
pap	quap	rap	sap
pas	quas	ras	sas
pat	quat	rat	sat
pav	quav	rav	sav
pax	quax	rax	sax
paz	quaz	raz	saz

tab	vab	wab	yab	zab
tac	vac	wac	yac	zac
tack	vack	wack	yack	zack
tad	vad	wam	yad	zad
taf	vaf	waf	yaf	zaf
tag	vag	wag	yag	zag
tal	val	wal	yal	zal
tam	vam	wam	yam	zam
tan	van	wag	yan	zan
tap	vap	wap	yap	zap
tas	vas	wack	yas	zas
tat	vat	wam	yat	zat
tav	vav	wav	yav	zav
tax	vax	wax	yax	zax
taz	vaz	waz	yaz	zaz

ă	ĕ	ĭ	ŏ	ŭ
bad	bed	bid	bod	bud
bag	beg	big	bog	bug
hat	hen	hit	hot	hut
pan	pen	pin	pop	pun
sat	set	sit	sock	sun
Nat	net	nit	not	nut
ban	Ben	bin	Bob	bun
bat	bet	bit	box	but
pat	pet	pit	pot	pup
pack	peck	pick	pock	puck
dad	deck	did	dock	dud
tack	Ted	tick	tock	tuck
hack	heck	hick	hock	huck
ham	hem	him	hop	hum
Dan	den	din	Don	duck
lag	leg	lip	log	lug
lack	let	lick	lock	luck
ran	red	rib	rob	rub

Deb	beck	bell	Ed	egg	Jeff
web	deck	cell	bed	beg	
	heck	dell	fed	keg	
	neck	jell	led	leg	
	peck	fell	Ned	Meg	
		mell	red	peg	
		sell	Ted		
		tell	wed		
		well			
		yell			

cell
sell

	end			
Ben	bend	bet	gem	hex
den	fend	get	hem	Rex
Jen	lend	jet		Tex
fen	mend	met	hep	vex
hen	rend	net	pep	
Ken	send	let		
Len	tend	pet	yes	
men	wend	set		
pen		vet	Bess	
ten		wet	less	
yen		yet	mess	
zen				

Bess fed Jack an egg.
Let Jeff tell Ben.
Can Rex tell Pam?
Deb had an egg.
Dad let Ken get wet.
Deb has a red pen.
Send Len an ax.
Lend Jen a pet.
Ben has a jet.
Rex fell.
Tell Bess yes.
Deb can yell.
Ted has a cat as a pet.
Get Jeff a keg.
Tex and Len set a net
Bess has less.
Ten men met.

beb	ceb	deb	feb
bec	cell	dec	fem
beck	cem	deck	fed
bed	cen	ded	fef
beg	cep	del	fel
bel	ces	dem	fem
bem	cel	den	fen
ben		dep	fep
bep		des	fess
bes		det	fet
bet		dev	fen
bev		dex	fex
bex			fez
bez			

heb	jeb	keb	leb
hec	jec	kec	lec
heck	jeck	keck	leck
hef	Jeff	ked	led
heg	jeg	keg	leg
hel	jel	kel	lel
hem	jem	kem	lem
hen	jen	ken	len
hep	jep	kep	lep
hes	jes	kes	less
het	jet	ket	let
hev	jev	kev	lev
hex	jex	kex	lex
hez	jez	kez	lez

meb	neb	peb	reb	seb
mec	nec	pec	rec	sec
meck	neck	peck	reck	sek
med	ned	ped	red	sed
mef	nef	pef	ref	sef
meg	neg	peg	reg	seg
mel	nel	pel	rel	sell
mem	nem	pem	rem	sem
men	nen	pen	ren	sen
mep	nep	pep	rep	sep
mess	ness	pes	res	ses
met	net	pet	ret	set
mev	nev	pev	rev	sev
mex	nex	pex	rex	sex
mez	nez	pez	rez	sez

teb	veb	web	yeb	zeb
tec	vec	wec	yec	zec
teck	veck	weck	yeck	zeck
ted	ved	wed	yed	zed
tef	vef	wef	yef	zef
teg	veg	weg	yeg	zeg
tel	vel	wel	yell	zel
tem	vem	wem	yem	zem
ten	ven	wen	yen	zen
tep	vep	wep	yep	zep
tes	ves	wes	yet	zes
tet	vet	wet	yev	zet
tev	vev	wev	yex	zev
tex	vex	wex	yez	zex
tez	vez	wez	yes	zez

if	in	is	it	ill
Jif	bin	his	bit	Bill
miff	fin	sis	fit	bill
tiff	pin		hit	dill
	sin		lit	fill
	tin		pit	gill
	win		quit	hill
			sit	Jill
			wit	mill
				pill
				quill
				rill
				sill
				till
				will

ib	ick	ic	id	ig	im
bib	Dick	bic	bid	big	dim
fib	hick		did	dig	him
rib	kick		hid	fig	Jim
	lick		kid	gig	Kim
	Mick		lid	jig	rim
	Nick		mid	pig	Tim
	pick		rid	rig	vim
	quick		Sid	Mig	
	Rick			wig	
	sick			zig	
	tick				
	wick				

ip	iss	ix	iz		
dip	hiss	Dix	fizz	quick	Phil
hip	kiss	fix	Liz	quit	Philip
kip	miss	mix	quiz	quip	
lip		nix		quill	
nip		pix		quiz	
pip		six			
quip		Rix			
rip					
sip					
tip					
zip					

ph		Ph

Quick Rick, fix it.
Tim bit his lip.
Nick is a sick kid.
Nick will get well.
Will Bill kiss Jill?
Will Bill tell Jill?
Sid will miss his pet pig.
His pig is big.
Jim is a big kid.
His hat fit him well.
Phil hid his hat.
Jack hid his ham in his hat.
Liz was sick and was fed in bed.
Mix it, fix it, and quit it.
Will Bill win Jill?
Is Jill ill?
Yes, Jill is ill.

| th |

th	at	that
th	an	than
th	e	the
th	em	them
th	en	then
th	in	thin
th	is	this

ba	th	bath
ma	th	math
pa	th	path
Be	th	Beth
wi	th	with

That man has a cat.
The cat is a big cat.
The cat is a thin cat.
This is his cat.
This is Beth.
Tell them that Rex is at bat.
The cat is in the bag.
Did Beth tell them that the cat is in
the bag?
Rick hid the bag with the cat.
The cat ran.
Let the cat dig in the sand.
The pig ran with the cat.
Dick ran with the bag in hand.
Phil is with Beth.
Then Beth ran with the hen.

ob	ock	od	of	og
Bob	hock	cod	off	cog
cob	dock	God		dog
gob	nock	mod		fog
mob	lock	nod		hog
rob	mock	rod		log
sob	pock	sod		
	rock	Tod		
	sock			
	tock			

tick-tock

om	on	op	ot	ox	oz
mom	Don	cop	dot	box	
Tom	Ron	hop	got	fox	
pom	son	mop	hot	pox	
	ton	top	not	sox	
	won		lot		
			pot		
			rot		
			tot		

pom-pom
Red Sox

The quick fox got on top of the box.
The red hen fell in the bath and got wet.
The Red Sox will win.
Yaz will win.
Tom is the son of Jack.
The dog ran with the cat.
The pot got hot.
Is the dog in the box?
The dog is not in the box.
Bob and Don sat on the dock.
Tell mom that Bob has the mop.
That fox is in the big tin box.
That box has a lock on it.
Quick, lock the box.
But the fox ran.

s		
cat	s	cats
dog	s	dogs
pet	s	pets
wig	s	wigs
pig	s	pigs
pill	s	pills
pot	s	pots
pan	s	pans
hand	s	hands

's		
Don	's	Don's hat.
Bob	's	Bob's dog.
Jack	's	Jack's pet.
Jill	's	Jill's cat.

es		
kiss	es	kisses
box	es	boxes
tax	es	taxes
fox	es	foxes

The man has ten cats and six dogs.
Jill has six hens.
Jim's pet pig is big.
Don kisses his mom.
Pam's cat is fat.
Ten pins.
Jack has six boxes of eggs.
Mom has ten pots and pans.
Rex's hat is red.
The dog ran with the foxes.

ub   ud   ug   ull   um   un   up
cub   bud   bug   cull   bum   bun   cup
dub   dud   hug   dull   gum   fun   pup
hub   mud   jug   gull   hum   gun
pub   mug   hull   mum   nun
sub   rug   full   sum   pun
tub   tug   bull   yum   run
                  pull   sun

us   ut   ux   uz
bus   but   lux   duz
fuss   cut   fuzz
Gus   gut
muss   mutt
pus   rut
        put

The dog dug in the mud and had fun.
Tom's dad put the pup in the tub.
Can Jack pull the big log up the hill?
Jack and Jill ran up the hill.
The red jug is full.
The dog got mud on the rug.
Bud's dog fell in the tub.
Gus put the mug on the rug.
Rick hugs his pup.
The sun was up at six.
The tub is full of mud.
The bug dug in the rug.
A big bull is in the pen.
Val put the mud in the bath tub.

bad	did	bed	bob	dud
dad	bid	deb	bod	dub
dab	bib	ded	dod	bud
bab	dib	beb	dob	bub

| sh | a sh   ash |

ash	esh	ish	osh	ush
bash	mesh	dish	gosh	gush
cash		fish		hush
dash		wish		rush
gash				
mash				
lash				
rash				
sash				

| bush |
| push |

| wash |

shack	shed	shin	shock	shun
	shell	ship	shop	shut
			shot	

| ch |

chap	check	chick	chop	chuck
chat	chess	chill		chug
	chet	chin		chum
	chex	chip		

| rich | much |
| | such |

| wh |

| what | when   whim
                                       whip
                                       which

cash	fish	chess
what	chop	shock
ship	shop	chuck
rich	much	shack
shut	rash	chug
dish	which	what
chill	shell	chin
wish	when	chex
rush	chick	which
when	such	ash
dash	shed	shot
mush	shun	chap
chum	chip	whip

Don had fish and chips.
Which dish is Dad's?
Which dish has the fish in it?
This dish is full of chips.
Pam sat on the deck of the ship.
Don has a chill. Bud has a rash.
Rick has cash and is rich.
Bud is his chum.
His chin is thin.
He hid the dish of fish in the shed.
The shop will shut when it is six.
When will Jim shut the shop?
Chuck is in the shack.
Dad has a chess set.
Chuck will wash the ship.
Pull the dog off the ship.

I am	I have
You are	You have
he is	he has
she is	she has
we are	we have
they are	they have

I was	I had
you were	you had
he was	he had
she was	she had
we were	we had
they were	they had

I have a cat.
She has a cat.
We had a cat and a dog.
They have six pets.
You have a pet pig.
Are you sick?
No, I am well.
She put the pup on the bed.
The pets were in the tub.
They were in the hut.
He has a rash.
Did you get sick?
No, I did not get sick.
Did she win?
Yes, she won.

is not	isn't
can not	can't
has not	hasn't
it is	it's
let us	let's
did not	didn't

Lesson 37

Is Bill sad?	Bill isn't sad.
Can they run?	They can't run.
Is this Peg's dog?	
This isn't Peg's dog.	
It's Jill's dog.	
Let's run.	
Has Peg a cat?	Peg hasn't a cat.
Did Jill run?	Jill didn't run.

hot-dog	hotdog
box-top	boxtop
zig-zag	zigzag
cat-nip	catnip
tick-et	ticket
hel-met	helmet
vel-vet	velvet
tom-cat	tomcat
gal-lop	gallop
les-son	lesson
nap-kin	napkin
tid-bit	tidbit
hab-it	habit
rap-id	rapid
gal-lon	gallon
can-did	candid
bas-ket	basket
bon-net	bonnet

ton-ic	tonic
mag-ic	magic
un-fit	unfit
gob-lin	goblin
rob-in	robin
chap-el	chapel
pic-nic	picnic
kid-nap	kidnap
lin-en	linen
vis-it	visit
rab-bit	rabbit
nit-wit	nitwit
viv-id	vivid
civ-il	civil
Nix-on	Nixon
len-til	lentil
pen-cil	pencil

egg-nog	eggnog
com-et	comet
pup-pet	puppet
up-set	upset
lock-et	locket
mim-ic	mimic
pub-lic	public
sun-tan	suntan
sud-den	sudden
hat-box	hatbox
sun-set	sunset
hat-rack	hatrack
bash-ful	bashful
den-tal	dental
un-til	until
hus-band	husband
wag-on	wagon

ex-it	exit
Phil-ip	Philip
riv-et	rivet
with-in	within
Cal-vin	Calvin
tab-let	tablet
pack-et	packet
rock-et	rocket
sock-et	socket
van-ish	vanish
pan-el	panel
Jap-an	Japan
ras-cal	rascal
cac-tus	cactus
cam-el	camel
Kev-in	Kevin
Kar-en	Karen
rib-bon	ribbon

rad-ish	radish
mas-cot	mascot
com-bat	combat
Pat-rick	Patrick
rel-ish	relish
lem-on	lemon
pock-et	pocket
traf-fic	traffic
bob-cat	bobcat
sig-nal	signal
lim-it	limit
li-quid	liquid
sat-in	satin
tun-nel	tunnel
rib-bon	ribbon
jack-et	jacket
pad-lock	padlock

Jill has a picnic basket full of hotdogs and relish.

Philip has a suntan.

Kevin is a rascal.

Karen and Ken will visit dad.

Calvin put the pencil in his jacket pocket.

Bill's mascot is a rabbit.

Don put a red ribbon on his cat's neck.

Mom has a red satin bonnet.

Peg's husband has a wagon.

The camel sat on the cactus.

Pam can mimic a puppet.

Deb has a red velvet sash.

Jim has a gallon of lemon tonic

Let's visit Patrick's dad.

A vivid sunset.

a as in all

Al	all	mall
Cal	ball	pall
gal	call	tall
Hal	fall	wall
pal	gall	yall
	hall	

Cal's pal Tim is tall. Did Hal fall?
Cal has the ball.
Cal hit the ball with the bat.
Philip sat on the wall.
His jacket is in the hall. Call Cal.
Tell Cal that his ball is in the hall.
Is the ball in his jacket pocket?
Yes, it is.

ng			
ang	ing	ong	ung
bang	bing	bong	hung
dang	ding	dong	lung
gang	king	gong	rung
hang	ping	pong	sung
pang	ring	song	
rang	sing	long	
sang	wing		
	zing		

ding-dong
Hong-Kong
wing-ding
sing-song
ping-pong

Deb sang a song.
Ron rang the bell.
The gang sang.
Tim is in Hong Kong.

Wash-ing-ton
Washington

fan	fanning	pack	packing
nap	napping	pick	picking
get	getting	yell	yelling
let	letting	sell	selling
set	setting	pass	passing
kid	kidding	sing	singing
rub	rubbing	ring	ringing
dig	digging	hang	hanging
rob	robbing	fix	fixing
shop	shopping	wish	wishing
ship	shipping	rush	rushing
run	running	wash	washing
call	calling	fall	falling

Jan is singing a song.
Bill is ringing the bell.
Ken is getting all wet.
Rick is kicking the ball.
Bob is calling his dog.
The cat is licking his leg.
Jack is yelling at Jill.
Mom is yelling at Bill.
Pat is packing his bag.
Cal is passing the ball.
Chuck is fixing the shack.
Tim is patting the cat.

| nd |

and	end	ond	und
band	bend	bond	fund
hand	fend	fond	
land	lend	pond	
sand	mend		
wand	rend		
	send		
	tend		
	wend		

| nt |

ant	ent	pent	unt
pant	bent	rent	bunt
rant	cent	sent	hunt
want	dent	tent	punt
	gent	vent	runt
	lent	went	
	Kent		

Bill is mending his tent.
Kent went hunting.
Jack went with Kent.
Tim is at the pond fishing.
Beth is fond of Kent.
Fishing is fun.
Rick has a fishing rod.
Bob lent Tom his fishing rod.
Bob wants his rod back.

er	her
let-ter	letter
bet-ter	better
hunt-er	hunter
lend-er	lender
send-er	sender
but-ter	butter
tend-er	tender
chat-ter	chatter
big-ger	bigger
sum-mer	summer
win-ter	winter
sis-ter	sister

Butter is better.
Ken has a sister.
Summer is better than winter.
Her hat is bigger.
Bill sent a letter.
Her dad is a hunter.

nk	nc	nch

hank   sink   bunk   ranch
honk   mink   lank   bench
hunk   ink   kink   inch
rank   junk   fink   pinch
link   dunk   lunch
pink   rink   punch
wink   tank   zinc

Lesson 47

Hank put cash in the bank.
Bob put gas in the tank.
Beth put the dish in the sink.
Bill had a hunk of junk.
Dan sat on a bench.
Dad has a ranch.
Tim had lunch.

ct	ft	pt	xt
act	aft	apt	next
fact	left		text
pact	lift		
tact	gift		
duct	raft		

Bill got a raft as a gift.
He left his raft at the pond.
The raft is big.
Can Bill lift the raft?
The fact is that he can't.
Jack will get the next gift.
Beth can act.
Can the raft sink?
It can't sink.

sk	sp	st	
ask	asp	last	must
bask	lisp	best	fast
cask	gasp	fist	lest
desk		rest	list
risk		bust	west
task		cast	rust
mask		dust	gist
dusk		jest	mist
		vast	vest
		test	zest
		just	pest
		mast	nest

Jim sat at his desk.
Can Jill pass the test?
Beth did her best.
Bill went west.
Bob did his task.
Hank can run fast.

lb	**ld**	**lf**	**lk**
bulb	held	elf	milk
	meld	self	silk
	geld	golf	bulk
		gulf	sulk

bald

calf
half

talk
walk

lm	**lp**	**lt**	
elm	help	melt	pelt
helm	gulp	belt	felt
film	yelp	jilt	cult
	pulp	quilt	hilt
		tilt	

mp

camp	bump	damp	jump
limp	romp	lamp	dump
lump	hump	pump	

Lesson 53

tch

itch	pitch	catch	witch
match	hitch	dutch	fetch
patch	etch	hutch	retch
botch	latch	hatch	ditch

watch

Jack has an itch.
The cat is in the ditch.
Pam lit a match.
Dad has a watch.
Can the cat catch the fish?
Bill will pitch his tent at the camp.

dge

edge   badge   ridge   fudge
hedge   wedge   budge   lodge
ledge   Madge   hodge   podge

The cat sat at the edge of the
sink and did not budge.

nce   nse

fence   since   tense   dense
sense   mince   dance   hence
rinse   dunce   once

The cat sat on the fence.
Jack and Pam can dance.

match	bath	went
milk	jump	half
left	elm	hunt
ring	tint	dance
dust	rinse	with
dish	edge	hint
belt	bank	pitch
pest	act	rich
cash	ink	rust
fudge	help	fast
kept	much	test
pink	next	elf
lung	patch	fist
desk	hunt	witch
last	west	fond
lost	sing	send
melt	camp	bend
catch	itch	fence

con-test	contest
sand-wich	sandwich
sel-fish	selfish
rub-bish	rubbish
pol-ish	polish
den-tist	dentist
ab-sent	absent
pun-ish	punish
shop-lift	shoplift
af-ter	after
ob-ject	object
dust-pan	dustpan
con-duct	conduct
bath-mat	bathmat
fin-ish	finish
con-sent	consent
chop-stick	chopstick

bl

blab	bled	blink	block	blunt
black	blend	bliss	blond	blush
bland	bless		blop	
blank			blot	
blast				

br

bran	brick	bred	brunt
brand	brig	broth	brush
brash	bridge		
brat	brim		
brass	bring		
	brink		

cl

clan	clip	club	clod
clap	cliff	clump	clock
clamp	click	cluck	clop
class			clob
clasp			

cr

crab	crib	crud	crest
crack	crisp	crum	crop
cram		crush	
crank		crutch	
crass		crux	

dr

drab	dredge	drift	drug
draft	dress	drill	drudge
drag	drop	drink	drum
		drip	

dw

dwell

Lesson 61

fl

flab	flesh	flip	flock	flub
flash	fled	flit	flog	flunk
flack		flint	flop	flush
flag				
flat				
flap				
flax				

fr

Fran	Fred	frog	frill
France	fret	frost	
Frank	fresh	froth	
	French		

gl   **gr**   **gw**

glad	grab	Greg	Gwen
gland	grad	grid	
glass	gram	grim	
glen	grant	grin	
glib	grand	grub	
glob	grass	grudge	
gloss			
glum			
glut			

pl		pr	
plan	plot	prep	prince
plank	plug	prig	print
plant	pluck	prim	prod
plop	plum	prick	prom
	plus	prance	prompt

Lesson 64

sl

slab	sled	slosh
slack	slid	slot
slag	slick	slum
slam	slim	slop
slant	slip	slush
slap	slink	slump
slat	sling	slung
slash	slob	

shr	sm	sn

shrink	smack	snick
shred	smash	snip
shrimp	smell	snap
shrank	small	
shrunk	smog	
shrug	smug	

sp			spr

spam	spell	spit	spring
span	spend	spot	sprang
spank	spent	spun	sprung
spat	spill	spud	
speck	spin		
sped			

st			str
stab	stem	stink	strand
stack	step	stint	strap
stag	stub	stock	strep
stan	stick	stomp	string
stand	stiff	stop	strip
stank	sting	stuck	strut

Lesson 68

sw	sc	sk	scr
swim	scab	skid	scrub
swam	scalp	skill	scrunch
swell	scan	skim	scrod
swan	scant	skin	
swish	scat	skip	
swift	scuff	skit	
swamp		skunk	
switch			

tr

track	trek	trod	trunk
tram	trend	trot	trust
trance	trick	truck	
trap	trim	trudge	
trash	trip		

thr

thrall	throb
thrash	throng
thresh	thrush
thrift	thrust
thrill	

tw

twig
twin
twist
twit
twang
twelve
twitch

truck	jump	bless
skip	then	dutch
swift	spun	with
quick	slosh	pest
grudge	shrimp	dish
glass	shack	bank
blond	plum	king
fudge	prom	fond
dump	frill	act
task	flag	lift
sash	cliff	left
lisp	crux	kept
clasp	draft	trick
dwell	chest	France
clap	bridge	hitch
slack	edge	next
spring	golf	lunch
witch	elm	flash

God bless this land.
The cat sat still.
Bill had fudge with his lunch.
Patrick drank a glass of milk.
Gwen put cash in the bank.
Pam had a stiff neck.
Kenneth had shrimp for lunch.
The king of France was fat.
Frank is a prince.
The bus stop is on the bridge.
His skin has an itch.
Stan put the trash in the basket.
Fred sat on the grass.
The frog swam in the swamp.
A frog can jump and swim.
A skunk can jump and skip.

ă	ā
at	ate
hat	hate
fat	fate
mat	mate
rat	rate
Al	ale
pal	pale
Sal	sale
gal	gale
fad	fade
mad	made
man	mane
Jan	Jane
van	vane
cap	cape
gap	gape

ā as a-e

Abe	ace	age	ale	ape
babe	face	cage	bale	cape
	lace	page	dale	gape
	pace	sage	hale	tape
	race	wage	male	drape
	brace	stage	pale	grape
	grace		sale	scrape
	place		tale	
	space		stale	
	trace		whale	
			scale	

ate	ade	ake	ame	ane
date	fade	cake	came	cane
fate	made	fake	dame	Dane
gate	wade	bake	fame	Jane
hate	blade	Jake	game	lane
Kate	grade	lake	lame	mane
late	spade	make	name	pane
mate	trade	quake	same	sane
rate		rake	tame	crane
crate		take	blame	plane
grate		wake	flame	
plate		brake	frame	
slate		flake		
		shake		
		stake		

ache

bare	base	cave	daze
care	case	Dave	maze
dare		gave	craze
fare	safe	pave	graze
hare		save	
mare		wave	
rare		brave	
ware		crave	
share		grave	
stare		slave	

are

have

Jane can bake a cake.
When will Kate wake up and take a
  bath?
Dave has an ache in his hand.
Bill's rabbit is in a cage.
Kate is late.
Dave has a date with Kate.
Jane ate the cake.
When will Dave shave his face?
Jack fell in the lake.
Can Dave save Jack?
Yes, Dave is brave.
Dave gave Kate a locket.
This place is safe.
The cat hid in the cave.
His name is Jake.
Jake made a date with Jane.
Dave's face is pale.

$\bar{a}$ as $\underline{ai}$

aid	ail	air	Cain	bait
laid	bail	fair	gain	wait
maid	fail	hair	main	trait
paid	Gail	pair	lain	
raid	hail	chair	pain	aim
said	jail	Clair	rain	maim
	mail		vain	claim
	sail		brain	
	nail		chain	
	frail		drain	
	trail		plain	
			slain	
			Spain	
			stain	
			train	
			strain	

again
against

Jane paid ten cents at the gate.
Gail will wait in the rain for the train.
If the train is late, Gail will take a bus.
In Spain the rain falls on the plain.
Cain is waiting at the main gate.
If the train is late, take a plane.
"Fish or cut bait," said Bill.
Gail is washing her hair.
Jane is trimming her nails.
"If it rains, take the train," said Dave.
"It is raining," said Kate.
"Wait for Jane," said Dave. But Kate
    did not wait in the rain.
The mail is late.
Spring is in the air.

ā as ay and ey

bay	lay	clay	hey
day	may	gray	grey
Fay	nay	play	they
gay	pay	stay	obey
hay	ray	slay	
jay	say	tray	
Kay	way	sway	
		stray	

Lesson 78

Can Fay play with Kay?
They say that Fay may play with Kay.
Jay will play a game with Kay.
Fay will stay with Kay all day.
Jay fell in the hay.
They went that way.
They came late that day.
The day was grey.

$\bar{a}$ as ei and eigh

rein	weigh
vein	sleigh
veil	eight
heir	eighth
their	weight
beige	freight

Bill is eight.
Jack has eight cents.
Kay's hat has a veil.
Dave ate eight cakes.
The freight train came.
Can they weigh the freight?
Yes, they can weigh the freight on
 a scale.

face	dare	grade	trail
pain	brave	cake	age
way	brain	day	wait
plate	gate	weigh	made
cage	vein	play	shade
space	fake	they	ale
scrape	stain	say	take
paid	care	ache	ail
chair	brake	jay	raid
their	main	mail	eight
tail	flame	ate	ate
vale	rain	hate	vain
veil	rein	quake	vein

Lesson 81

vale	veil	vail
rain	rein	reign
hail	hale	
ate	eight	
made	maid	
tale	tail	
male	mail	
wait	weight	
way	weigh	
main	mane	
vain	vein	vane

pay-day	payday
rail-way	railway
air-plane	airplane
space-ship	spaceship
a-way	away
en-gage	engage
wait-ress	waitress
rain-ing	raining
en-slave	enslave
grate-ful	grateful
ex-plain	explain
com-plain	complain
mail-man	mailman
ink-stain	inkstain
em-brace	embrace
ob-tain	obtain

au and aw

haul	Maud	awe	bawl
maul	fraud	jaw	brawl
Paul	launch	law	crawl
Saul	staunch	paw	drawl
fault	cause	raw	hawk
vault	pause	saw	dawn
gaunt	taut	claw	fawn
haunt		draw	lawn
jaunt		flaw	pawn
		thaw	yawn
aunt		slaw	brawn
		straw	drawn

Lesson 84

Paul saw a spot on Saul's jaw.
Paul saw Maud sitting on the lawn.
The cat cut her paw.
They must obey the law.
Paul drank his milk with a straw.
The dawn came.

a as in ma and car

ma	pa	father	haha
mama	papa		

arc	bar	bard	ark	art	arm
ark	car	card	bark	cart	farm
arm	far	hard	dark	dart	harm
art	jar	lard	hark	mart	charm
	mar	yard	lark	part	
	par	barb	park	tart	carp
	star		spark	start	harp
			shark	chart	
			stark	quart	barn
			Clark	smart	darn
			mark		yarn

Mark has a red car.

"Park the car in the yard," said Mark.

Pam has a big jar of jam.

Beth has a part in a play.

Mark's farm has a barn.

Father went far away.

It is dark in the park.

"Start the car," said ma.

The dog will bark in the dark.

Pa's yard is full of junk.

If Mark's arm has an itch, scratch it.

Beth has a ball of yarn.

"If it rains, put the cart in the barn,"
   said father.

The shark ate the small fish.

Mark is smart.

Clark drank a quart of milk.

Mark can take apart his car.

Long ē as ee

bee	eel	heed	beep	beer
fee	feel	deed	deep	deer
gee	heel	feed	keep	jeer
Lee	peel	need	jeep	peer
see	reel	reed	peep	cheer
free	steel	seed	seep	queer
tree	wheel	weed	weep	steer
flee		breed	creep	
three		creed	sleep	
knee		greed	steep	
			sweep	

beet	beef			
feet	reef	deem	breeze	
meet		seem	freeze	be
greet	leek	teem	geese	he
sweet	meek	seen	cheese	me
tweet	seek	teen	Greece	we
sheet	week	queen	fleece	she
street	Greek	screen	sleeve	

been

I see the tree.
Can the tree see me?
She is a queen.
Is she the queen of Greece?
Yes, she is the Greek queen.
We ate beef this week.
Lee came in a jeep.
Will they sweep the street this week?
They will sweep the street at three.
He is free at three.
She is sweet.
I have seen the queen.
Lee will greet the queen.
Lee is up a tree.
The queen is on her feet.
He and Lee will cheer the queen.
We ate cheese this week.
She ate cheese and beef.
"Meet me next week," she said.

Long ē as ea

pea	eat	ear	deal	beam	bean
sea	beat	dear	heal	ream	dean
tea	feat	fear	meal	seam	Jean
flea	heat	gear	peal	team	lean
	meat	hear	real	cream	clean
bead	neat	near	seal		
lead	peat	rear	veal		heap
read	seat	sear	weal	stream	leap
leaf	cheat	tear	zeal		reap
	treat	year	steal		
	wheat				

each	beak	east	ease	eave
beach	leak	beast	tease	leave
peach	peak	feast	lease	heave
reach	bleak	yeast	cease	weave
preach	speak		crease	
teach	streak		peace	
			please	

sweat	bear	dead	steak
threat	pear	head	break
sweater	tear	lead	
	wear	read	
	swear	bread	
		deaf	

Jean had a dream.
She put cream in her tea.
Jean ate a meal of veal and peas,
   bread and butter, tea and cake.
Bill is at sea.
The sea is in the east.
Jean can hear the sea in a sea shell.
Jean will leave at three.
When will Jean eat her meal?
Each week Jean eats a peach.
A ship at sea was seen in the east.
The beach is neat and clean.
Bill is on the team this year.
Will he be on the team next year?
When next year is near, we shall see.
Jean sat in her seat.
The seat is in the rear.
The team will win this year.
The dog has fleas.
The cat is neat and clean.
When will we reach the beach?

Long ē as e-e

gene	here	eve	Pete
scene	mere	Steve	these
there	were		eye
where			

Where is Steve?
Steve is here.
Where were Pete and Steve?
Pete and Steve were here.
Here is where they were.
Where were they?
They were here and there.
"Sit here, not there," said Steve.
Steve and Jean were at the beach.
The sun was in Steve's eyes.
Pete and Eve were there at the beach.
Eve has grey eyes.
Steve has green eyes.
Pete had a tear in his eye.

Long ē as ie

niece   thief   pier   field   siege
piece   chief   tier   yield   fiend
        grief   pierce shield
                fierce   friend

Debbie Lassie Blondie
Jackie Ronnie   receive
Minnie Connie
Vinnie

Debbie and Ronnie sat on the pier.
Jackie is Connie's friend.
Vinnie and Ronnie are friends.
Lassie ran in the field.
The thief ran away.
Vinnie ran after the thief.
The field is wet and green.
The sun is fierce.
Jackie shields her eyes from the sun.
Connie has a niece.
Her name is Minnie.

Long ē as y

Abby	daddy	taffy	baggy	Billy
Tabby	caddy	daffy	saggy	Sally
Libby	paddy	jiffy	Maggy	silly
lobby	Teddy	puffy	foggy	Molly
Debby	muddy	stuffy	Peggy	Polly
baby	study		muggy	chilly
			Twiggy	daily

mammy	Danny	Harry	messy	Betty
mommy	Denny	carry	sissy	batty
mummy	Fanny	Barry	fussy	catty
tummy	Benny	Perry	easy	fatty
Tommy	Jenny	Terry		city
Timmy	Lenny	merry	busy	nutty
Jimmy	Kenny	hurry		pity
Sammy	penny	sorry	hazy	
	bunny	Gary	lazy	pretty
happy	funny	marry	crazy	
pappy	sunny	berry	dizzy	candy
peppy		cherry	fuzzy	handy
poppy	money	very		sandy
puppy	any	furry		
	many	worry		

Billy was silly.
Taffy was daffy.
Mommy was happy.
Daddy was very merry.
Danny ate candy.
Kenny felt dizzy.
The lobby was stuffy.
The day is hot and muggy.
The bunny is funny.
Larry is dizzy.
Debbie is pretty.
Betty is pretty.
Jerry is in a hurry.
The day was chilly and foggy.
Perry is sorry.
Gary hasn't any money.
The city is hilly.
The day was sunny.
Daddy was busy.
Can Perry carry Barry?

baby	babies	lobby	lobbies
berry	berries	cherry	cherries
city	cities	bunny	bunnies
puppy	puppies	candy	candies
penny	pennies	hurry	hurries
marry	marries	study	studies

Lesson 96

tea	easy	queen	steer	eel
week	jeep	reach	greasy	ease
fear	tree	sweet	hear	clear
niece	he	sea	meat	city
beet	key	field	steal	beach
see	please	she	feet	read
dear	gear	study	meet	tease
here	near	Pete	chief	feel
she	thief	treat	cheer	peace
greet	mean	need	bean	seat
these	we	eve	weep	breeze
sleep	leaf	leap	creep	street

The street is neat and clean.

Lee's feet need rest.

She feels very sleepy.

"Meet me at the beach," Betty said.

Where is the beach?

The beach is near the city.

"Please teach me to read," Pete said to his teacher.

There is a breeze near the sea.

We can sleep on the beach and feel the sea breeze.

There are trees near the sea.

There are three peach trees in that field.

Steve can reach a peach with ease.

It is easy to read this page.

The cherries are sweet.

"For Pete's sake, hurry up," said Jean.

We will be back at the beach next week.

"Did Lee hear me?" asked Jean.

Long ī as i-e, y, ie

I am	by	die
I can	my	lie
I take	why	pie
I had	try	tie
I ran	dry	
I have	cry	
	spy	
	fly	
	fry	

ice	ike	ide	ime	ine
dice	bike	bide	dime	dine
lice	dike	hide	lime	fine
mice	hike	ride	mime	line
nice	like	side	rime	mine
vice	Mike	tide	time	pine
price	pike	wide	chime	vine
slice	spike	bride	crime	wine
twice	strike	chide	grime	brine
spice			prime	shine
			slime	spine
			clime	swine
			climb	thine
				twine
			rhyme	shrine

ile	ire	ive	ife	ipe	ise
bile	dire	dive	life	pipe	rise
file	fire	five	rife	ripe	wise
mile	hire	hive	wife	wipe	
Nile	mire	jive	strife	gripe	tribe
pile	sire	live		swipe	bribe
tile	tire	chive	knife	stripe	
vile	wire	drive			size
smile	spire	strive			prize
while		thrive			

give
live

I like ice cream.   I can ride a bike.
I can fly a kite. I ate a slice of pie.
I like rice. I like spice on my rice.
I like to smile.
What time is it ? It is five o'clock.
It's nice to ride a bike.
It's nice to drive a car.
I won a prize.
Her doll can cry like a baby.
Let's play hide and seek . I feel fine.

Long ī as igh

high	fight	tight
sigh	light	bright
thigh	might	fright
	night	slight
	right	flight
	sight	

The light was bright.
The price is right.
The night was chilly.
Is the price high?
Yes, the price is very high.
The fire is bright.
Land is in sight.
The bright lights of the city are a sight
    at night.
Mike was in a prize fight.
Mike fights with all his might.
The sky is bright.

ough and augh

ought	fought	caught
bought	sought	taught
brought	thought	daughter
		slaughter

though

I bought candy and gum.
Paul caught the ball.
He thought the ball was fast.
Dad taught a tennis lesson.

Lesson 102

gh as f

rough	laugh	draught
tough	laughing	
cough	laughter	

Dad has a cough.
Mom gave him a cough drop.
The steak was tough.
Mike made Billy laugh.
The sea was rough.

Long ō as o-e

obe	oke	ole	ome	one
robe	coke	hole	dome	bone
	joke	mole	home	cone
ode	poke	pole	Rome	lone
code	woke	role		tone
mode	broke	sole	come	zone
rode	choke	whole	some	phone
	smoke			
ote	spoke	oze	soul	one
note	stoke	doze		done
vote	stroke	froze		none
quote			ove	once
			cove	gone
			dove	
ope	ore	ose	rove	
cope	bore	dose	wove	
dope	core	hose	clove	
hope	fore	nose	drove	
pope	more	pose	grove	
rope	tore	rose	stove	
slope	sore	chose		
	yore	close	dove	
	chore		love	
	store		glove	
	swore		shove	
	shore		move	

My nose is sore.
My home is in Rome.
I spoke on the phone.
I had an ice cream cone.
I love a joke.
Tell me a funny joke.
One more time.
Once upon a time.
The stove is hot.
The dog ate the bone.
Perry wore a bath robe.
Jean woke up. Then she woke me up.
A rose is a rose. A rose smells nice.
Dad drove home.
He drank some Coke.
"Come home," he said.
Dad ate something for lunch.
Betty loves to talk on the phone.
Tell me more.
I sent Kathy a note.
The note was in code.

Long ō as oa

oat	oak	oar	load	boast
boat	soak	roar	road	coast
coat	cloak	soar	toad	roast
goat	coal	board	foam	toast
moat	goal	hoard	roam	
float	loaf	broad	Joan	
gloat	soap			

The car is on the road.
He bought a loaf of bread.
Joan ate a roast beef sandwich.
The soap can float.
Dad bought coal for the stove.
Jan and Joan had oatmeal.
Mom has tea and toast each day.
Dad bought a big boat.
The boat floats on the lake.
Joan wore her red coat.

Long ō as ow

bow	sow	crow	snow	shown
low	tow	flow	own	flown
row	know	grow	blown	known
mow	blow	show	grown	bowl

Joan wants to grow up.
The snow fell last night.
I know what I want.
Dad wants to own a car.
Bill wants his own boat.
Bob wants to row his boat.
Go slow in the snow.
I know the way home.
Jack will mow the lawn after lunch.
Mom gave the cat a bowl of milk.
Dad and Mike like to go bowling on
    Sundays.
Mike has grown up.
We saw a TV show.

Long ō as in old

old	hold	host	oh	only	boss
bold	mold	most	go		loss
cold	sold	post	no		moss
fold	told		so		toss
gold		cost	quo		
		lost	yo-yo		

The old home was cold.
"Hold my hand," she said.
"Go home," I told him.
He was lost. He had sold his home.
I know what he told her.
In winter it is cold most of the time.
Bob sold his gold ring.
I told him so. Dad sold his boat.
It had cost him a lot of money.
"It was only money," he said.
He is the only one I know with a boat.
But most of the time he stays home.
"Go slow. There is ice on the road," said Dad.

| too | do
to
two
who
you
youth | young |

Do you know who went to the phone?
Did you do what you were told?
The two of you must know what to do.
Who do you think you are?
Do you know who you are?
You are young.
You are too young to go alone.
The box is two feet high.
It is too big.
Give it back to him.
What shall I do?
Go to the man who sold it to you.

oo as in good food

coo	food	boon	boom	coop	cool
boo	mood	moon	doom	loop	fool
moo	goof	noon	broom	hoop	pool
too	proof	soon	room		drool
woo	roof	spoon	loom	sloop	spool
zoo	boob		zoom	snoop	school
	brood			stoop	

loose	boot	root	booth	ooze
noose	coot	toot	tooth	
moose	hoot	zoot	smooth	snooze
choose	loot			

good	hoof	book	nook	cookie
hood	wool	cook	brook	cookies
wood	foot	hook	crook	
stood	soot	look	shook	door
		took		floor
boor			spook	
poor				
moor				

Joan and Jane went to the zoo.

The zoo was too far from home.

Jane took a book with her.

Joan wore a wool coat.

Soon they will go to school.

The pool was cool, but the food was good.

Betty can cook good food.

Jim stood at the door and took a look.

Look at Betty's room. It's so neat.

"Open the door," said Pam. "I have cookies and
   milk."

The door is made of wood.

Barry sat on the floor. He took a snooze.

It's noon. Time for lunch.

Betty has too much to do this afternoon.

The broom is in Mike's room.

Go to his room and get it.

He took the broom.

Soon it will be noon.

Read a good book.

ould as ood in wood

could	could not	couldn't
would	would not	wouldn't
should	should not	shouldn't

I would go if I could.
He should go if he could.
Couldn't I go?
He could go, but not the two of you.
I would like to go.
I would like to see my father.
But should I go?
No, you should stay.
Should he go to school?
He shouldn't go to school if he has a cold.
I wouldn't go if I had a bad cold.
If I were sick I would stay in bed.
Would you?
Yes, I would.

ow and ou as in cow and ouch

bow	owl	down	bower	browse
cow	cowl	gown	cower	crowd
how	fowl	town	power	
now	howl	brown	tower	
pow	jowl	clown	flower	
sow	growl	crown		
vow		drown		
wow		frown		

ouch	loud	ounce	bound	count
couch	proud	bounce	found	fount
pouch	cloud	pounce	hound	mount
vouch		trounce	pound	
touch		noun	round	
			sound	

house	out		wound	our
louse	bout		ground	hour
mouse	lout	bough		sour
douse	pout	plough	wound	flour
blouse	clout	drought		
	trout			four
	doubt	rough		your
	shout	tough		
	mouth	enough		

How did the cow get out of the house?

A mouse let her out.

"I found the cow near the house," brother
said.

They heard a loud sound.

The house fell down.

"Ouch," said the clown.

The clown ran out of the house.

They went down town.

It took an hour to find the cow.

The cow was in a crowd, then she went
around the tower.

How now brown cow? Will you come
home?

"Not now," said the cow. "Bow wow," said
the dog.

A cop came to the house. "Your cow is
in town," he said.

The clown chased the mouse round
and round.

oy as in boy,   oi as in oil

boy	oil	coin	noise	hoist
coy	boil	join	poise	foist
joy	coil	loin		moist
Roy	foil	void		
soy	soil	joint		
toy	toil	point		choice
Joyce	broil			
Royce	spoil			

poi-son	poison	joy-ful	joyful
oil-y	oily	boy-ish	boyish
an-noy	annoy	broil-ing	broiling

Roy gave the toy to Joyce.
The cat likes to annoy Joyce.
Roy wants to join a club.
He has a choice of two clubs.
Joyce has a jar of coins.
Roy has a ball-point pen.
The water is about to boil.
The soil is moist.

Long ū as u-e

use	cube	dude	cuke	mule	dune
fuse	lube	Jude	duke	rule	June
muse	Rube	nude	juke	yule	tune
	tube	rude	Luke		prune
fume	dupe	crude		cure	cute
plume	huge	prude		pure	jute
Bruce					lute
				sure	mute
					brute
					chute
					flute

June can play a tune on the flute.
Luke sat on the sand dune.
June ate a prune.
Luke rode on a mule.
June is cute.
The duke is a prude.
The cloud was huge.
Luke put a dime in the juke box.
Is there a cure for a cold?
We are not sure.
If there is a cure, let's use it.
Bruce has a tube of tooth paste.
Dad put a fuse in the fuse box.
It's never nice to be rude.

Long ū as ue and ui

cue	blue	queue	juice
due	clue		fruit
hue	flue		bruise
	flu		cruise
Sue	glue		
	true		

Sue had prune juice at breakfast.

Is it true that Sue has the flu?

Yes, it's true.

Take a cue from Sue. When you have
   a cold, eat lots of fruit and drink
   lots of juice.

Sue's dress is blue.

Bruce has a tube of glue.

He will use the glue to fix a toy.

Long ū as ew and eu

dew	blew	grew	feud
few	brew	stew	deuce
Lew	chew	view	
mew	clew	threw	
new	crew	knew	
news	drew		
pew	flew		
sew			

June has a new dress.
What's new?
The news is good.
Good news is always nice.
Tell me the good news.
Lew is having beef stew.
I knew the news was good.
Sue likes to chew gum.
She grew an inch.
Luke threw a stone.
He threw it far.
Lew drew a cat in his sketch pad.

er, ir, or, ur and ear

her	nerve	sir	squirt	fur	urn
germ	serve	fir	birth	cur	burn
term	verve	bird	mirth	urge	turn
Bert	terse	firm	thirst	splurge	hurt
pert	verse	gird	smirk	surge	curse
fern		girl	quirk	curl	nurse
clerk		flirt		hurl	purse
jerk		dirt		lurk	curve
		shirt		Turk	

earn	work	birth-day	birthday
learn	word	thirst-y	thirsty
yearn	worm	tur-nip	turnip
heard	worst	tur-key	turkey
search	worth	ex-pert	expert
earth		home-work	homework

The girl wants to be a nurse.

It is her birthday.

Bert held the bird and heard it sing. The
  bird is thirsty.

Willy likes to learn new words. Sue likes to
  learn words that rime.

Word rimes with bird.

Curve rimes with nerve.

words ending in le

able	babble	dazzle	tattle	ample
cable	bubble	fizzle	turtle	sample
fable	pebble	drizzle	single	simple
table	apple	wiggle	jingle	dimple
stable	grapple	wriggle	jungle	pimple
idle	paddle	battle	bangle	temple
rifle	faddle	bottle	dangle	fumble
trifle	saddle	cattle	bungle	bumble
stifle	fiddle	little	juggle	humble
eagle	riddle	settle	struggle	tumble
beagle	raffle	kettle	strangle	handle
title	ruffle	brittle	tittle	candle

silent t: hustle, bustle, rustle, wrestle

He ate a little apple. He threw a pebble.
She had a little dimple. He sat at the table.
He had a pimple on his dimple.
She was nimble with a thimble.
The bottle was brittle.
The candle was on the table.
Can a beagle chase an eagle?
Can a turtle play a fiddle?
Are you able to handle a paddle?
The drizzle was a fizzle.
There was a battle in the jungle.

ph as f

Ralph	phone	physical	telephone
Phil	phony	physics	telegraph
Philip	phonics	pharmacy	photograph
Philadelphia	photo	Phoenix	graphic
	phase	philosopher	emphasis
	phrase	philosophy	emphatic

Lesson 121

ce, sc, ci, si, ti, xi, su, tu as sh, ch, zh

nation	special	capture	measure
station	racial	rapture	pleasure
ration	facial	fracture	treasure
notion	crucial	picture	leisure
motion			
potion	musician	question	
fraction	physician		
action		fusion	issue
traction	atrocious	confusion	tissue
	ferocious		sure
patient	conscious		insure
patience	obnoxious		assure
			fissure
mission	conscience		
fission			

kn as n

knee	knit	knack	know
kneel	knitting	knock	known
kneeling	knitted	knob	knowing
knelt		knuckle	knowledge
		knickers	knight

Lesson 123

mb as m

dumb	lamb	climb	plumber
numb	bomb	climbing	plumbing
crumb	bombing	climbed	
thumb	bombed	comb	tomb
		combed	
		combing	

bt as t : debt

Lesson 124

silent h

hour	ghost
honor	ghastly
honest	ghetto
heir	ghoul

wr as r

write	wring	wry	wreath
wrap	wrote	wretch	wrestle
wrong	wrench	wrought	wrestling
wreck	wrist	wretched	wrestled
wrack	wrath	wriggle	wrestler
writer	writing	written	

Lesson 126

st as s   ft as f

castle	wrestle	often
listen	wrestler	soften
moisten	whistle	softener
nestle	whistler	
hasten	listener	

Lesson 127

ch as k   ps as s

Christ	chorus	chlorine	scheme
Christian	choral		schedule
Christmas	chord		school
	chemist		scholar
character	chemistry		scholastic
	chronic		psychic
	chronicle		psyche

y as short i

cyst	gymnast	gymnasium
gym	mystic	mystery
hymn	system	syllable
Lynn	symbol	sympathy
myth	symptom	synonym
nymph	rhythm	hysteric
	physic	hypnosis
	syrup	cylinder
	lyric	typical
	Cyril	tyranny
	syntax	synthetic
	Phyllis	mystical

TEACHER'S MANUAL

Pages 131 - 150

ALPHA-PHONICS TEACHER'S MANUAL

INTRODUCTION

This course of instruction will enable any teacher or tutor to teach reading to anyone who needs to learn it: beginning readers of all ages or poor readers in need of retraining. The method is based on a thorough analysis of the English writing system, how it works, and how best it can be taught.

Written English is a purely alphabetic system, regardless of what we may think of its many eccentricities and irregularities. An alphabet, by definition, is a set of graphic symbols that stand for the irreducible speech sounds of a particular language. Therefore, all of our written words stand for spoken sounds, no matter how irregular the spellings may be.

We must not forget that the invention of the alphabet is based on one of man's greatest discoveries: that all of spoken language is composed of a relatively small number of different speech sounds. (In English, only 44!)

This is one of the great discoveries that has enabled man to do much more with much less. Instead of wrestling with a writing system using thousands and thousands of symbols representing thousands of individual ideas and concepts, as in Chinese or Egyptian hieroglyphics, man could create a writing system using less than fifty symbols to handle an entire language.

It is vitally important to understand the difference between an alphabetic writing system and an ideographic one. The latter uses graphic symbols to represent ideas, concepts, feelings, actions, things, etc. An ideographic system is basically independent of any particular language although many of its symbols may represent specific words of a language. In an ideographic system language is used to interpret the symbols. Precision and accuracy are therefore hard to achieve with an ideographic system.

An alphabetic system, on the other hand, is a sound-symbol system used merely to represent on paper a particular spoken language. The spoken words stand for the ideas, concepts, feelings, etc., while the written words are mere graphic representations of the spoken words. Therefore, in an alphabetic system, the relationship between written and spoken language is one of precision and exactness. The spoken word may be subject to interpretation, but the written word is an exact representation of a specific spoken counterpart. Thus alphabetic writing can also be a tool of thought, for the thought process uses the spoken language for its development.

The invention of the alphabet, which took place about 2000 B.C., not only made hieroglyphics and every other ideographic system obsolete, it permitted a tremendous expansion of vocabulary because now there was a writing system that could easily accommodate it. The greatest works of the ancient world have come down to us through alphabetic writing: the Iliad. the Odyssey. the Greek dramas, the Bible. Without the alphabet, man's intellectual and spiritual development would have been seriously retarded. So we must regard the alphabet with great awe, respect, and even love. It Is civilization's prize possession.

It stands to reason that a thorough knowledge and understanding of the English alphabetic system will enable a pupil not only to read well, but also to spell well. We often forget that our writing system is a two-way process: to be used both for reading **and** writing, decoding and encoding; and a pupil must become proficient in both in order to be truly literate.

Knowledge alone, however, does not lead to reading fluency. To gain fluency requires all of the techniques used in developing a skill to the point where it seems effortless: practice, frequent use, drill, review, etc.

This course of instruction makes full use of all of these proven techniques of learning. Moreover, it teaches in a logical, systematic way facts about our alphabetic system which are usually taught rather haphazardly if at all. And it makes these facts operating knowledge for the student who wishes to learn to spell accurately and enlarge his or her vocabulary.

No one denies that the English alphabetic system is somewhat complex. But its complexity is hardly an excuse for not teaching it.

For far too long, teachers of reading have avoided the difficulties of our alphabetic system by teaching sight vocabularies, whole-word configurations, context clues, and incidental phonetic clues. While such methods may produce some initial success on the primary level, they are, in the long run, injurious because they violate the basic nature of our writing system and are not in harmony with its principles. They do not provide the student with a fundamental understanding of the symbolic system we use in reading and writing, an understanding which he or she must have in order to become truly literate.

It was Dr. Samuel T. Orton, the world's foremost expert on dyslexia, who first warned educators that the look-say, whole-word method could be harmful. He wrote in *Educational Psychology* in 1929 that the whole-word method "may not only prevent the acquisition of academic education by children of average capacity but may also give rise to far-reaching damage to their emotional life."

ALPHA-PHONICS was created to make it unnecessary for any teacher to expose a child to teaching methods that can be harmful.

OUR ALPHABETIC SYSTEM

The English alphabetic system may be complex, but it can be taught and it ought to be taught. We have an alphabetic system of great range and flexibility. Our spellings reveal much about the history and development of our language, and once the eccentricities of the system are learned, they are learned. They do not change. The reward for learning this system is to have for one's personal use and enrichment the entire body of our published literature. Such a literary treasure is indeed the priceless inheritance of everyone who can read.

Our English alphabetic system is complex for a variety of reasons: (1) it uses 26 letters to stand for 44 sounds; (2) it uses five vowel letters to stand for 21 vowel sounds; (3) many consonant letters stand for more than one sound; (4) some sounds, particularly the long vowel sounds, are represented by more than one spelling; (5) the invasions of foreign languages have enriched English but complicated its spellings (6) pronunciations have changed over the centuries but the spellings have not, creating many irregularities.

Despite all of this, our system is more than 80 percent consistent or regular, with most of the irregularities consisting of variant vowel spellings.

In devising this instruction program, we have taken all of the above into account. Therefore, we start out by teaching the pupil the short vowels, which are the most regular in spelling, in conjunction with the consonants. Then we teach the consonant blends - final blends first, then the initial blends. Last, we teach the long vowels in their great variety of spelling forms.

Thus we proceed from the simple to the complex in easy stages, giving the pupil plenty of practice and drill along the way. The pupil learns to read and spell in an orderly, systematic, logical way, as well as to pronounce the language with greater accuracy.

To some teachers this will seem like an overly academic way to teach reading. And it is, on purpose, because we want the pupil to learn to enjoy using his or her mind.

In teaching someone to read English, we must decide what should come first: learning the alphabetic system or enjoying inane stories with lots of irregular sight words. The latter may seem to be much more fun for teacher and pupil; but does it accomplish what we want to accomplish? If our goal is high literacy, it does not.

We know from experience that the pupil will derive much deeper satisfaction by learning the alphabetic system first, because it will give him or her much greater overall reading mastery in a shorter period of time.

Competency and skill are the two most important ingredients of self-confidence, and self-confidence is the cornerstone of self-esteem. Learning to read is the pupil's first real exposure to formal education, and a positive attitude can be instilled in the young mind by how we approach the subject at hand.

It is obvious that one learns faster and better when the knowledge one is expected to acquire is organized in such a way as to make its acquisition as easy as possible. This is the concept behind ALPHA-PHONICS. Our aim is to provide the pupil with the kind of basic knowledge that will become the solid foundation of all his or her future academic work.

Of course, no instructional program teaches itself. Its success depends a great deal on the teacher. This program has a good deal of flexibility and provides many ways to measure the pupils' progress. But since pupils vary greatly in their prior knowledge and capabilities, the teacher in some instances will have to tailor the instruction to the individual pupil.

While we have organized this course in a certain order to make sure that what should be learned is learned, we have also done this to make the teaching of reading as easy for the teacher as possible. We therefore advise the teacher to read this book in its entirety before using it.

133

TEACHING THE ALPHABET

The fastest and most efficient way to teach the alphabet is to have the child repeat it after you in alphabetical order while you point to the letters. Thus the child learns the alphabet both orally and visually at the same time. Usually the oral learning will be faster than the visual, since the oral alphabet when repeated often enough is learned almost like a melody or a poem. The alphabet lends itself easily to this kind of learning since it can be broken up into rhythmical and rhyming lines as follows:

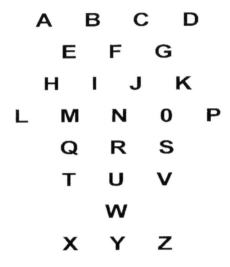

It will take some time, before the child's visual learning catches up with his or her oral knowledge. Indeed, some children learn to recite the alphabet perfectly long before they are able to identify all of the letters at random. This is perfectly normal since the child has had much oral practice learning to speak the language. However, now he is required to do highly precise visual learning which may take some getting used to, especially if the child has had little exposure to print.

Children with photographic memories will learn visually much faster than those not so favorably endowed. The slowest learners will be those with weak visual memories. These children will benefit most from simple alphabetic exercises, such as repeating the letters at random, several at a time, as in the Prereading Alphabet Exercises, (p. 159).

Both oral and visual learning of the alphabet should be accompanied by kinesthetic learning, that is, by having the pupil draw the letters in both capital and lower-case forms. Drawing the letters will help the child learn their different shapes more thoroughly. A lined notebook should be used by the pupil for doing this work in class and as homework.

Another effective way for the child to learn to identify letters at random is to ask him or her to pick out specific letters from advertisement print matter in newspapers and magazines. In this way the pupil learns to recognize the letters in different sizes and type faces. This is also a good way to check on the child's vision.

Pictures are not necessary in teaching the alphabet if you do it in the systematic manner prescribed in this program. The picture the child should be looking at is the **letter itself**, not an apple or a bumblebee, or an elephant.

Pictures are a distraction that can only delay learning the alphabet directly as a set of graphic symbols. We make this point because shortly after the letters are learned, the pupil will be taught to identify them with speech sounds, and this is very crucial.

A letter is a symbol of a sound. It is not the symbol of anything else.

The letter is supposed to stimulate the mouth, lips, and tongue to make particular sounds. It is not supposed to make the pupil think of an apple or an elephant. He or she must translate groups of letters into speech, and the pupil will be able to do this more readily the better he or she associates the letters with sounds.

A word of caution: When a pupil is having uncommon difficulty learning or mastering any phase of the instruction, do not become impatient and do not scold. Analyze and try to pinpoint the cause of the difficulty. You may simply have to take more time than you thought necessary. Some students take a year to master what others can master in a month. Remember, the goal is not to win a race but to teach a person to read - no matter how much time it takes to do the job well.

TEACHING THE LETTER SOUNDS

Assuming that the pupil has learned the alphabet, we are now ready to teach the letter sounds. The pupil's knowledge of the alphabet does not have to be letter perfect before we move on to this next phase, for the simple reason that the student will learn the letters better as they are used.

When you are ready to teach the letter sounds, you might explain to the student something about how and why the alphabet was invented. Older students are usually quite fascinated to learn that the entire English language is made up of only 44 irreducible speech sounds. Try, if possible, to appeal to the learner's intellectual curiosity. You never know what kind of a response you will get.

Pupils are very sensitive about their ability to learn. This is particularly true of remedial students whose self-esteem has been badly battered by failure. A learning block or handicap, is not a reflection of basic intelligence. We all know of highly intelligent people who have trouble doing simple addition. We also know that many so called dyslexics are very bright and articulate. Therefore, always appeal to a pupil's basic intelligence.

When teaching younger pupils the letter sounds you might simply say: "Now we are going to learn the sounds the letters stand for so that you can put the letters to work for you. Each letter stands for a different sound. You will be able to read words by knowing the sounds the letters stand for."

The essence of what you want to convey to the pupil is that letters have meaning - they stand for sounds - and that the letters in a written word tell the reader how to say it.

In teaching the letter sounds, it is important to convey the idea that the distinct sounds of our language can be isolated and represented by written symbols. Obviously the alphabet was invented by someone who spoke clearly and heard clearly and could distinguish between the fine differences of speech sounds, between the **t** and the **d**, between **s** and **z**, **m** and **n**, short **a** and short **e**. But a pupil's attunement to speech sounds may not be very sharp. In fact, some pupils may articulate very poorly and require a good deal of work to improve their pronunciations. Therefore, spend as much time as is needed to sharpen your pupil's attunement to the isolated, irreducible speech sounds of our language as you teach the letter sounds. Be sure to pronounce all words clearly.

The alphabet is a tremendously exciting invention based on a great discovery: that all of human language is composed of a small number of irreducible speech sounds. In teaching the alphabet, you can convey to your pupil the excitement of this great discovery and the marvelous invention based on it "Did you know that every word you speak can be put down on paper?" you tell the pupil. That's exciting. "And that's what you are going to learn to do - to put down on paper every sound of speech you make."

Thus you've established the concept of a set of written symbols representing speech sounds. This is the association you want to establish in the pupil's mind: that letters on paper stand for sounds that he can make with his voice, and that the sounds he makes can be put down on paper by way of letters representing them.

SOME PRACTICAL SUGGESTIONS

This book has been designed to be used as both a tutoring and a classroom text. If the classroom teacher has only one copy of ALPHA-PHONICS, then the pupils should be provided with lined notebooks in which to copy lessons from the board. Ideally, each pupil should have his own copy of ALPHA-PHONICS plus a notebook in order to facilitate the assignment of homework. This would also reduce the need for time-consuming board work by the teacher and costly duplicating.

Tutored pupils should also, whenever possible, have their own copies of ALPHA-PHONICS for homework and reference use. The pupil should also have a lined notebook for practicing cursive, spelling exercises, vocabulary lists, and sentence writing. It is advisable to assign some written homework after each tutoring session. The purpose of homework is to speed up the acquisition, retention, and improvement of skills. The amount of homework should depend on the amount of time between sessions.

Although the lesson instructions have been written from a classroom viewpoint, a tutor will find them easily adaptable for one-on-one teaching. Simply substitute pupil for class.

ISOLATING THE LETTER SOUNDS

In articulating the letter sounds, the best way to isolate a consonant sound is to listen to what it sounds like at the end of a word; then lift it from the rest of the word. By doing so, you will minimize injecting a vowel element.

This can be done with consonants **b, ck, d, f, g** (as in **tag** and **large**), **k, l, m, n, p, r, s, t, v (ve), x z (ze), sh, ch, th.** Consonant **c** stands for the **k** sound before vowels **a, o** and **u;** it stands for the **s** sound before vowels **e** and **i.** The letter **q** is always followed by **u** and is pronounced as if it were **kw.**

Some consonants - **h, j, w, y, wh** - do not appear as consonants at the ends of words. These can also be articulated in isolation with just the barest hint of a vowel element.

By pronouncing the isolated sounds as purely as possible, the pupil will be able to understand what we mean by an irreducible speech sound.

ORDER OF LESSONS

LESSON 1: Have the pupils turn to Lesson 1 in their textbooks. Start by telling the class (student) that you are now going to teach the sounds the letters stand for. "When you learned the alphabet, you learned the names of the letters. Now you're going to learn the sounds the letters stand for. Let's start with the first sounds. Now listen to the sound I make." Make a short **a** sound. (Short **a** is the **a** in **cat**) "Did you hear that sound?" Make it again and ask the class to repeat it after you. "That sound is not a word all by itself, but you hear it and say it often in many words. Can you say it again?" After the class repeats the short **a** sound and hears you repeat it, print the letter **a** on the blackboard. "The letter **a** that you see on the board and in your books stands for the sound you just made. It is called the short **a** sound. Now I am going to say five words with that sound in it, words that you use every day: **am, an, as, at, ax**" Print them on the board as they appear in the book. Give examples of how each word is used in a spoken sentence, so that the class understands that they are words. A word is the smallest unit of speech that has meaning. "The short a sound all by itself doesn't mean anything. But a sound that means something is a word. **Am, an, as, at, ax** are all words because they have meaning.

"Now each of these words has two letters in it. Can you name the letters?" Have the class spell each word, saying the word after it is spelled. Spelling a word means naming its letters in proper left-to-right sequence. "Now if the words each have two letters and each letter stands for a sound, how many sounds does each word have?" Repeat the word **am** slowly. Write and say the short **a** sound; then write and say the word **am** just below it "Do you hear the difference between **a** and **am?** When we say **am,** we add another sound to the **a.** What is the sound we added to the **a** in the word **am?**" Say the **m** sound as it is said in the word **am.** (To correctly isolate this consonant sound, listen to what it sounds like at the end of a word; then lift it from the rest of the word. By doing so you will minimize injecting a vowel element.) After you've made the **m** sound, ask the class: "Did you all hear it? Can the class say it?" After the class says the **m** sound, tell them that the letter **m** stands for the **m** sound. "So if we want to write the word **am** we must write **a-m,** because these are the letters that stand for those sounds."

137

Repeat the procedure for **an, as, at, ax.** In this instance teach the **s** as soft **s.** Just as the vowel letters represent more than one sound, some consonants also have variant sounds. But at this stage, we are teaching only the sounds used in the words presented in the textbook Have the pupil print these words, say them, spell them. (This may also be a good time to start teaching cursive writing. For instruction on introducing cursive, page 156.) In any case, make sure that the pupils understand that each word has two sounds and that they can match the right sound with the right letter. Point out how the name of each letter, except **a** in this instance, gives them a hint of the sound each letter stands for. Exaggerate the sounds so that the class can hear them distinctly and learn to recognize them when heard.

When you are convinced that the class knows these letter sounds thoroughly, tell them that there are two kinds of letters in the alphabet - vowels and consonants. **A** is a vowel and **m, n, s, t and x** are consonants. The other vowels are **e, i, o, and u.** All the rest are consonants, although **y** is sometimes used as a vowel. Explain that the vowels are the most powerful letters in the alphabet, because you can't have a word without one. Consonants need vowels in order to make words. They can never stand alone. You needn't elaborate at this point, suffice it merely to establish the fact that there are two classes of letters: vowels and consonants.

By now the class has learned a great deal. They are beginning to hear words with a greater awareness of their different sounds, and they have seen how these different sounds are represented in their books by alphabet letters. They see that the letters are printed from left to right in the same sequence as they are spoken. The five words can also be printed on cards and flashed to the class in short drills to help develop quick recognition.

LESSON 2: Review all of the material taught in Lesson **1.** When that is done, print the word **am** on the board. Tell the class that you are going to make a new word by adding **S** to the beginning of it. Ask if anyone can figure out what that new word is. The word is the name **Sam.** Ask them how many sounds are in that word. Have them identify the three sounds in the order they are printed. Explain that we use a capital **S** in the word **Sam** because it is a proper name and all proper names begin with capital letters. Repeat this procedure with the other words in the lesson. With the word **has** identify the sound the letter **h** stands for.

LESSON 3: Have the class study all of the words in the lesson and read them aloud. Now tell them that they know enough words to be able to write their first sentences: **Sam sat. Sam has an ax.** Explain that a sentence begins with a capital letter, whether the first word is a name or not, and that it ends with a period. Define a sentence as a complete thought.

LESSON 4: Teach the sound the letter **d** stands for to make the word **ad.** Expand **ad** to **dad.** Introduce the sound of the letter **w.** Put the **w** in front of **ax** and see if the class can figure out the word **wax.** Place **D** before **an** to make **Dan.** Have the class read the two new sentences.

LESSON 5: By now the class should begin to understand the principle behind alphabetic word building, how each letter's sound is used in writing words Have the class read the words in their columns. By using all of the letters known by the class, their reading vocabulary has been expanded to 25 words. Point out that the word **was,** while in the **as, has** spelling family, is pronounced **wuz.** This is an irregular pronunciation. Thus the class has been made aware that there are irregularities in the system.

LESSON 6: Have the class read the sentences made up of the words they know. Explain that we place a question mark at the end of a sentence that asks a question. Have the pupils write the sentences as part of cursive instruction. Also, use the sentences in dictation exercises.

LESSON 7: Add **d** to **an** to make **and.** Expand **and** into **hand, sand, land.** Explain that **nd** is a blend of two consonant sounds and make sure that the pupils can hear and identify the four sounds in each of these four-letter words. Introduce the sound of **l** in making **land.** Ask the class if they can hear the difference between **an** and **and.** Show how **and** is used. Have the pupils read the sentences and write them with capital letters at the beginning.

LESSON 8: Introduce **l** as a final consonant, and capital **A** in **Al.** Introduce **c** (as in **cat**), **g** (as in **gas**), **j, l,** and **n** as initial consonants. Expand the pupils' reading vocabulary to include the words in this lesson. Make up practice sentences if desired.

LESSON 9: Introduce consonants **p, t** (initial) **r, v, w, y, z.** Make sure that the pupils can articulate each irreducible consonant sound. Make up practice sentences. Have the pupils read all of the new words and discuss the meanings of those they might not know.

LESSON 10: Drill review of known short **a** words in rhyming columns or spelling families. Correct all errors in reading. Spend as much time as necessary to develop proficient knowledge of these consonants. Have pupils sound out words they find difficult.

LESSON 11: Introduce **ck** as standing for the **k** sound. Expand the pupils' reading vocabulary as indicated. Introduce **qu** with the word **quack.** With **ck** the pupil learns that sometimes two letters will stand for one sound. Therefore, although the word **back** has four letters, there are only three sounds in the word.

LESSON 12: Introduce the word **a,** as in **a cat, a hat,** etc. It has the same meaning as **an,** but is used before a word that starts with a consonant. Like **an,** it is an indefinite article meaning one.

LESSON 13: Practice sentences. These can be read and written.

LESSON 14: Short **a** and consonant drill columns. Introduce letter **k** and its sound on page 19. The columns include many nonsense syllables which will later turn up in many multisyllabic words. Have the class read these columns aloud.

LESSON 15: Introduce the rest of the short vowels by comparative sounding and having the pupils read the sets of words with the different vowel sounds. Teach the pupils to pronounce the five short vowel sounds in isolation. The aim of the lesson is to get the pupil to associate the right vowel sound with the right vowel letter.

LESSON 16: Short **e.** Expand the pupils' reading vocabulary to include all of the words in this lesson. Discuss the meaning of words the pupils may not know. Point out that **c** also stands for the **s** sound as in **cell.** (The letter **c** stands for the **k** sound before vowel letters **a, o, u.** It stands for the **s** sound before vowel letters **e, i.**) The letter **g** at times also stands for the **j** sound before vowel letters **e** and **i,** as in **gem.**

LESSON 17: Practice sentences with short **e** words.

LESSON 18: Short **e** drill columns. They include many nonsense syllables that will later turn up in many multisyllabic words. The purpose of these drills is to reinforce knowledge of the consonants. Note that initial consonant **c** should be sounded as **s** in this exercise, and sounded as **k** in the final position. **C** before short **e** is sounded as **s.**

LESSON 19: Short **i.** Expand the pupils' reading vocabulary to include the words in this lesson. Introduce **ph** as another form of **f** in teaching the name **Phil.** Also see if the class can figure out their first two-syllable word: **Philip.**

LESSON 20: Short **i** practice sentences.

LESSON 21: Introduce the consonant digraph **th.** Articulate the sound it stands for and have the class repeat it. Then show what happens when **th** is added as an initial consonant and final consonant to known syllables. A consonant digraph is not a blend. We simply do not have enough letters in our alphabet to stand for all of our separate sounds. So sometimes we use two letters to stand for one irreducible sound. That is the case with **th.** Just as there is a hard **s** and a soft **s,** there is a hard **th** as in **thin** and a soft **th** as in **the.** Make sure the pupils pronounce each word correctly.

LESSON 22: Practice sentences with **th** words.

LESSON 23: Short **o.** Articulate the short **o** sound as in Lesson 15 and expand the pupils' reading vocabulary to include the words in this lesson. Note that **off** and **dog** have irregular pronunciations as well as **son, ton,** and **won.**

LESSON 24: Short **o** practice sentences. These include irregular words which should be pronounced as they are normally spoken.

LESSON 25: Introduce plural **s, es,** and apostrophe **s.** Explain how they are used: **s** and **es** for plural, apostrophe **s** for ownership.

LESSON 26: Practice sentences with plural **s, es,** and **'s.**

LESSON 27: Short **u.** Articulate the short **u** as in Lesson 15 and expand the pupils' reading vocabulary to include the words in this lesson. Note the irregular pronunciations of **full, bull, pull,** and **put.** By pointing out the irregulars, we affirm the consistency of everything else.

LESSON 28: Short **u** practice sentences. Make sure that the irregular words are pronounced as they are normally spoken.

LESSON 28a: If the pupil often confuses **b** with **d,** use these drill columns for practice.

LESSON 29: Introduce the consonant digraph **sh.** This is another single consonant sound represented by two consonant letters. Expand the pupils' reading vocabulary to include the words in this lesson. Note the irregularly pronounced words: **bush, push, wash.**

LESSON 30: Introduce consonant digraph **ch.** Expand the pupils' reading vocabulary to include the words in this lesson.

LESSON 31: Introduce consonant digraph **wh.** Articulate it carefully to distinguish it from simple **w.** Expand the pupils' reading vocabulary to include the words in this lesson.

LESSON 32: Review of short-vowel words with consonant digraphs. Give spelling tests to check pupils' knowledge.

LESSON 33: Practice sentences with consonant-digraph words.

LESSON 34: At this point introduce our two most common verbs, **have** and **be.** The pupil is already familiar with the words **am, is, was, has, had.** The words **have, am, they, were, you** are common but irregular words. The pupil already knows the sounds of their consonant letters, so teach these words as sight words. The sole purpose of this lesson is merely to expand the pupil's ability to read more interesting sentences. However, these words will be more thoroughly studied when encountered later in their own spelling families.

LESSON 35: Practice sentences using the words learned in Lesson 34.

LESSON 36: Contractions. Introduce the concept of contractions by showing how the pupil uses them in his everyday speech. Now show how they are written with the use of an apostrophe.

LESSON 37: Practice sentences with contractions. Point out the two uses of the apostrophe: in **isn't** denoting contraction; in **Peg's** denoting possession.

LESSON 38: There are many two-syllable words made up of simple short-vowel syllables. Have the pupils read the words first as hyphenated, then as wholes. That will convey to them how multisyllabic words are constructed. This is also a good time to test spelling. Go around the class and have each pupil try a word. This will indicate to you how well the pupils have learned the alphabetic principle. With slower pupils, go back to previous review lessons to improve their knowledge and proficiency.

LESSON 39: Practice sentences with two-syllable words learned in Lesson 38.

LESSON 40: Introduce the sound of **a** as in **all** and other double **l** words. Explain that the letter **a** stands for more than one sound. The pupil already knows the short **a** sound. This is the second **a** sound he is being introduced to. Use practice sentences.

LESSON 41: Introduce the **ng** consonant blend. Explain that a blend is bringing two sounds closely together. They sometimes seem like one sound, but when you listen to them carefully, you can hear the two separate sounds. Expand the pupils' reading vocabulary to include the **ng** words in the lesson. Teach the word **Washington** as shown. Notice the doubling of the final consonant on most short-vowel words when adding **ing.**

LESSON 42: Practice sentences with **ing** words.

LESSON 43: Review of final consonant blend **nd.** Expand the pupils' reading vocabulary with the **nd** words in this lesson. Introduce final consonant blend **nt.** Teach the **nt** words in the lesson. Note irregular pronunciations of **want** and **wand.** The letter **w** seems to alter the sound of short **a** whenever it precedes it.

LESSON 44: Practice sentences with **nd** and **nt** words.

LESSON 45: Introduce the syllable **er,** which is really a variant **r** sound. (The **e** in **er** is also considered a distinct variant vowel sound. But it is too minor to be taught as such.) Show how by adding **er** to many already known words, the pupil can expand his reading vocabulary to include many new words. Have the pupils read the short practice sentences and make up others.

LESSON 46: Introduce final consonant blends **nk, nc, nch.** Expand the pupils' reading vocabulary to include the words in this lesson.

LESSON 47: Practice sentences using words with the final consonant blends learned in Lesson 46.

LESSON 48: Introduce final consonant blends **ct, ft, pt, xt.** The pupils' reading vocabulary can be expanded to include the words in this lesson. Also, have the pupils read the practice sentences.

LESSON 49: Introduce final consonant blends **sk, sp, st.** Expand the pupils' reading vocabulary to include the words in this lesson. Also, have the pupils read the practice sentences. Make up other sentences if desired.

LESSON 50: Introduce final consonant blends **lb, ld, lf, lk.** Expand the pupils' reading vocabulary to include the words in this lesson. Note the irregular words: **bald, calf, half, talk, walk.** Make up practice sentences using the words in this lesson, including some of the irregular ones. Limit the sentences to words and sounds learned through Lesson 50.

LESSON 51: Introduce final consonant blends **lm, lp, lt.** Expand the pupils' reading vocabulary to include the words in this lesson. Make up practice sentences if desired.

LESSON 52: Introduce final consonant blend **mp.** Expand the pupils' reading vocabulary to include the words in this lesson. Make up practice sentences if desired.

LESSON 53: Introduce final consonant blend **tch.** The **tch** blend is really a spelling variant of the consonant digraph **ch. Rich** rhymes with **itch,** and **much** rhymes with **dutch.** Expand the pupils' reading vocabulary to include the words in this lesson. Explain to the class that there are many variant spellings of the same sounds in English. That's what makes our alphabetic system so rich and flexible. Just as **k** and **ck** stand for the same sound, so do **ch** and **tch** at the ends of words. Explain that **ch** sometimes also stands for the **k** sound. We shall take that up in Lesson 127. Have pupils read the practice sentences. Note the irregular pronunciation of **a** in **watch.**

LESSON 54: Introduce final consonant blend **dge.** It is a variant spelling of the soft **g.** Expand the pupils reading vocabulary with the words in this lesson. Have the pupils read the practice sentences and make up others if desired.

LESSON 55: Introduce final consonant blends **nce** and **nse.** Expand the pupils reading vocabulary with the words in this lesson. Note that **once** rhymes with **dunce.** Use practice sentences.

LESSON 56: Review of final consonant blends in one-syllable short-vowel words. See how many your pupils can read.

LESSON 57: Many two-syllable words are made up of simple short-vowel words and syllables combined with other short-vowel words and syllables, some of which have final consonant blends and consonant digraphs. Have your pupils try to figure out these words on the basis of what they have been taught thus far. This is a good way to find out how well your pupils have progressed, who among them needs some practice and drill, and who are ready to move ahead.

NOTE: If you are impatient to begin teaching some long vowel words, you can skip to Lesson 72 and start with long **a.** Lessons 58-71 teach the initial consonant blends. Return to them at intervals until you complete them.

LESSON 58: Introduce initial consonant blends **bl, br.** Expand the pupils' reading vocabulary with the words given. Make up practice sentences if desired.

LESSON 59: Introduce initial consonant blends **cl, cr.** Teach the words given. Make up practice sentences if desired.

LESSON 60: Introduce initial consonant blends **dr, dw.** Expand the pupils' reading vocabulary to include the words in this lesson. Make up practice sentences if desired.

LESSON 61: Introduce initial consonant blends **fl, fr.** Expand the pupils' reading vocabulary to include the words in this lesson. Make up practice sentences if desired.

LESSON 62: Introduce initial consonant blends **gl, gr, gw.** Expand the pupils' reading vocabulary to include the words in this lesson. Make up practice sentences if desired.

LESSON 63: Introduce initial consonant blends **pl, pr.** Expand the pupils' reading vocabulary to include the words in this lesson. Make up practice sentences if desired.

LESSON 64: Introduce initial consonant blend **sl.** Expand the pupils' reading vocabulary to include the words in this lesson. Make up practice sentences if desired.

LESSON 65: Introduce initial consonant blends **shr, sm, sn.** Expand the pupils' reading vocabulary to include the words in this lesson. Make up practice sentences if desired. Note that **shr** is made up of a consonant digraph and a consonant.

LESSON 66: Introduce initial consonant blends **sp, spr.** Note that **spr** is a blend of three consonant sounds. Expand the pupils' reading vocabulary to include the words in this lesson. Make up practice sentences if desired.

LESSON 67: Introduce initial consonant blends **st, str.** Note that **str** is a blend of three consonant sounds. Expand the pupils' reading vocabulary to include the words in this lesson. Make up practice sentences if desired.

LESSON 68: Introduce initial consonant blends **sw, sc, sk, scr.** Note that **scr** is a blend of three consonant sounds. Expand the pupils' reading vocabulary to include the words in this lesson. Make up practice sentences if desired.

LESSON 69: Introduce initial consonant blends **tr, thr, tw.** Note that **thr** is made up of a consonant digraph and a consonant. Expand the pupils' reading vocabulary to include the words in this lesson. Make up practice sentences if desired.

LESSON 70: Review of short-vowel words with initial and final consonant blends.

LESSON 71: Practice sentences with words learned through Lesson 70. These are good test sentences to evaluate the progress of your pupils. Where you detect weak spots, go back to previous drills for reinforcement. However, move as rapidly as you can into the next series of lessons which take up the long vowels.

LESSON 72: The long **a** sound. Explain to the class that they have learned all of the short vowel sounds and how to read them, plus all of the consonants and consonant blends. Now they are going to learn the long vowel sounds. Explain that the long vowel sounds are pronounced the same as their letter names: **a, e, i, o, u.** We start with **a.** Ask the pupils if they can hear the difference between the words **at** and **ate.** Write them on the blackboard to show them what they look like. Explain that the silent **e** changes the short **a** to a long **a.** Explain that both words have only two sounds each, but that the word **ate** has three letters, one of which seems to be silent. Explain that it is not really silent, however, because both the **a** and the **e** separated by a consonant stand for the long **a** sound. Now under the word **at** write the words **hat, fat, mat, rat.** Under the word **ate** write **hate, fate, mate, rate.** Ask the pupils to explain what happened when you added an **e** to the words under **at.** Next, write the words **Al** and **ale.** Ask the class if they can read these words. If the pupils have heard of ginger ale, they will be familiar with the word **ale.** Under **Al** write **pal, sal, gal,** and under **ale** write **pale, sale, gale.** Ask the pupils to read these words. The words in this lesson are arranged as described above. Have the pupils read the rest of the words in the two columns, comparing sounds and spellings.

LESSON 73: Expand the pupils' reading vocabulary to include these long **a** words. Explain that in **age** the **g** is soft as opposed to **g** in **get** and **gal.** Note the three irregular words and their particular spelling families: **ache, art, have.** Explain that the **ch** in **ache** stands for the **k** sound; **are** rhymes with **car, have** rhymes with **mav.** Seeing these irregularities in the context of their spelling families, the pupils should conclude that irregularities are few and that they tend to affirm the consistency of everything else.

LESSON 74: Practice sentences with long **a** words as spelled **a** /consonant/ **e.**

LESSON 75: Long **a** as spelled **ai.** Explain to the class that there is more than one way to write long **a.** The second most common way is **ai.** Teach these **ai** words in their spelling families. Note irregular words **said, again, against. Said** rhymes with **red. Again** rhymes with **Ben.** The **ai** in **against** is pronounced as the **ai** in **again.**

LESSON 76: Practice sentences with long **a** words.

LESSON 77: Long **a** as **ay** and **cy.** Explain that there is a third and fourth way in which long **a** is spelled. Teach the **ay** and **ey** words. Note that the long **a** in these spelling forms occurs at the ends of words. Also note that the **ey** words represent a small minority of this group and that they are really irregulars.

LESSON 78: Long **a** as **ay** and **ey** practice sentences.

LESSON 79: Long **a** as **el** and **eigh.** Introduce these two additional ways of writing long **a.** They are less common than **a**/consonant/**e, ai, ay and ey,** but they include some frequently used words. Expand the pupils' reading vocabulary to include these words. Their use is demonstrated in the practice sentences. Point out, incidentally, that we know three ways to write long **a (ey, ei, eigh)** in which the letter **a** does not appear.

LESSON 80: Review of long **a** words in their spelling varieties. Explain that these spellings are permanent and that simply because there are six ways to write long **a** doesn't mean that we can spell words any way we like. We must always use the spelling that is correct.

LESSON 81: There are many words (homonyms) that sound alike but have different spellings and meanings. This is true of many long **a** words, and we can see why it is useful to have more than one way to write long **a.** It helps us identify the meaning of the word by knowing its spelling. For example, **ate** and **eight** sound exactly alike, but their spellings are so distinctly different that we know which meaning to apply immediately on sight. Have the pupils learn the words in this lesson. However, do not expect them to learn them well at this point. They will learn them much better after seeing them in the context of a sentence or paragraph in future reading. The purpose of the lesson is mainly to make the pupils aware that such a phenomenon exists and that variant spellings of the same sound are therefore quite useful.

LESSON 82: Two-syllable words with long **a** spellings. See how many your pupils can figure out. This is a good way to test their knowledge and progress and to see where additional review and practice drills are necessary. Make up practice sentences with these words if desired.

LESSON 83: Introduce the **aw** vowel sound as spelled **au** and **aw.** Teach the words in this lesson. Note the irregulars **awe, aunt.**

LESSON 84: Practice sentences with **au, aw** words. Make up additional sentences if needed.

145

LESSON 85: Introduce the sound of **a** as in **ma** and **car.** This is the fourth sound of **a** we have learned. The first three were short **a,** long **a,** and **a** as in all. Expand the pupils' reading vocabulary to include the words in this lesson. Note irregular **quart.**

LESSON 86: Practice sentences with **a** as in **ma** and **car.**

LESSON 87: Introduce the long **e** sound in its most common spelling form **ee.** Expand the pupils' reading vocabulary by teaching the **ee** words in their spelling families. Explain that the **kn** in knee stands for the **n** sound, that been rhymes with **sin,** and that **be, he, me, we** and **she** are all long **e** words.

LESSON 88: Practice sentences with **ee** words.

LESSON 89: Long **e** as **ea.** The second most common way of writing long **e** is **ea.** Expand the pupils' reading vocabulary to include the words in this lesson. Note the variety of irregular words in the **ea** group. In **sweat, threat, dead, head, lead, read, bread, deaf** the **ea** is pronounced as a short **e. Bear, pear, tear, wear,** and **swear** all rhyme with **air. Steak** and **break** rhyme with **cake.** Note that **tear** as in **teardrop** and **tear** meaning **rip** can only be correctly read in context. The same is also true of **read** (present tense) and **read** (past tense).

LESSON 90: Practice sentences with **ea** words.

LESSON 91: Long e is also spelled **e**/consonant/**e** as in the words in this lesson. Note the exceptions: **there, where, were, eye. Eye** is one of the most irregular words in our written language. However, even in this case, the **y** suggests a long **i.** The distinctive spelling of the word makes it an easy one to learn. Have the pupils read the practice sentences.

LESSON 92: Long **e** is also spelled **ie** as in the words in this lesson. Note the exceptions: **friend** and **receive.** Friend rhymes with **blend,** and **receive** reminds us of the rule "**i** before **e** except after **c**" Have the pupils read the practice sentences.

LESSON 93: Long **e** as **y.** This particular spelling form is usually found at the end of words as shown in the lesson. Note these irregular pronunciations: **pretty** rhymes with **city; busy** rhymes with **dizzy; money** rhymes with **sunny. Any** and **many** rhyme with **penny.**

LESSON 94: Practice sentences with long **e** as **y** words.

LESSON 95: Plural **ies.** Teach the class that when a word ending in long **e** as **y** is made plural, the correct spelling is **ies.** Have the class study the words in this lesson. Make up practice sentences.

LESSON 96: Review of long **e** words in variant long **e** spellings.

LESSON 97: Practice sentences with long **e** words.

LESSON 98: Introduce the long **i** sound and its several variant spellings: **i**/consonant/**e, y, ie.** Teach the class the long **i** words in this lesson in their spelling families. Note the spelling of **climb, knife,** and the irregular pronunciations of **give** and **live.**

LESSON 99: Practice sentences with long **i** words.

LESSON 100: Long **i** as **igh.** This archaic spelling is used in some of our most common words. Expand the pupils' reading vocabulary to include the words in this lesson. Also, have the pupils read the practice sentences.

LESSON 101: Introduce the archaic spelling forms **ough** and **augh,** representing the **au** sound, by teaching the common words in this lesson. Note the irregular pronunciation of **though.** These words are generally easy to learn because of their distinctive spelling. Have the pupils read the practice sentences and make up others if desired.

LESSON 102: ntroduce **gh** as **f.** Expand the pupils' reading vocabulary to include the words in this lesson. Note that the **au** in **laugh** and **draught** stands for short **a;** the **ou** in **rough** and **tough** stands for short **u.** Use practice sentences.

LESSON 103: Introduce the long **o** sound. The most common spelling for long **o** is **o**/consonant/**e.** Expand the pupils' reading vocabulary to include the words in this lesson. Point out the irregular words in their particular spelling families: **dove, love, glove, shove, move, come, some, whole, one, done, none, once, gone, soul.**

LESSON 104: Practice sentences with long **o** words spelled with **o**/consonant/**e.**

LESSON 105: Long **o** as spelled **oa.** Expand the pupils' reading vocabulary to include the words in this lesson. Have pupils read practice sentences.

LESSON 106: Long **o** as spelled **ow.** This is the third way long **o** is spelled. Expand the pupils' reading vocabulary to include the words in this lesson. Have pupils read the practice sentences.

LESSON 107: Long **o** as in **old.** Expand the pupils' reading vocabulary to include the words in this lesson. Note the irregulars. Have the pupils read the practice sentences.

LESSON 108: Common irregular words. It is best to teach these words in the context of the practice sentences. Explain that **to, too,** and **two** all sound alike but have different meanings. **Too** is regular, while **to** and **two** are not.

LESSON 109: Introduce the two sounds of **oo** as in **good food.** Expand the pupils' reading vocabulary to include the words in this lesson. Note irregular **door** and **floor.**

LESSON 110: Practice sentences with **oo** words.

LESSON 111: Introduce the archaic spelling **ould** which sounds like **ood** in **wood.** Expand the pupils' reading vocabulary to include these common words and their contractions. Have the pupils read the practice sentences.

LESSON 112: Introduce **ow** and **ou** as in **cow** and **ouch.** Explain that **ow** stands not only for long **o** in one set of words (see Lesson 106), but also stands for the **ow** sound as in **cow** in another large set of words. Most of these words are quite common, and therefore the pupil will have little trouble determining which sound applies. The irregulars in this group are **touch, wound** (injure), **four, your, rough, tough, enough.**

LESSON 113: Practice sentences with **ow, ou** words as in **cow** and **ouch.**

LESSON 114: Introduce the **oy, oi** sound as in **boy** and **oil.** Expand the pupils' reading vocabulary to include the words in this lesson. See if the pupils can figure out the two-syllable words. Have them read the practice sentences and make up more if desired.

LESSON 115: Introduce the long **u** sound and its most common spelling, **u - e.** Give examples by pronouncing such words as **use, June, cube, mule.** These words are spelled with the **u** followed by a consonant and **e.** Expand the pupils' reading vocabulary with the words in this lesson. Note the **sh** pronunciation of **s** in **sure.** Have pupils read practice sentences.

LESSON 116: The long **u** is also spelled **ue** and **ui.** Expand the pupils' reading vocabulary with these **ue, ui** words. Have pupils read practice sentences.

LESSON 117: The long **u** is also spelled **ew** and **eu.** Expand the pupils' reading vocabulary with the words in this lesson. Note the irregular pronunciation of **sew** which rhymes with **grow.** Have the pupils read the practice sentences.

LESSON 118: The **er** sound group as spelled **er, ir, or, ur, ear.** Note the general interchangeability of spellings in this sound group. The correct spellings, however, are best learned in spelling families. Have the pupils read the practice sentences. Also have them figure out the two-syllable words.

LESSON 119: Many common two-syllable words in English have an **le** ending in which the **l** sound terminates the word with only the slightest hint of a vowel sound preceding it. Expand the pupils' reading vocabulary with the words in this lesson. Note the silent **t** in the words indicated. Also have the pupils read the practice sentences.

LESSON 120: The pupil has already been introduced to **ph** as representing the **f** sound. This lesson has additional words for the class to become familiar with.

LESSON 121: Words in which **ce, sc, ci, ti, xi, su, tu** stand for **sh, ch, zh.** These words are of Latin derivation, but their pronunciations have been anglicized. Note **zh** as a separate and distinct consonant sound without its own spelling form.

LESSON 122: The pupil has already been introduced to several words in which the **kn** represents the **n** sound, as in **knee.** Familiarize your pupils with the other **kn** words in this lesson.

LESSON 123: There is a spelling group in which **mb** stands for the **m** sound. Expand the pupils' reading vocabulary with the words in this lesson. Also note the **bt** as **t** in **debt.** The **b** in these words is commonly referred to as silent **b.** However, this is somewhat erroneous, for it is the combination of letters that stands for the **t** sound, not any of the letters alone.

LESSON 124: The silent **h.** There probably was a time when the **h** in these words was pronounced. But now it is not. Familiarize the pupils with these words. In the **gh** words, teach **gh** as representing the **g** sound as in **go.**

LESSON 125: Introduce consonant digraph **wr** as representing the **r** sound. Expand the pupils' reading vocabulary with the **wr** words in this lesson.

LESSON 126: Introduce **st** as **s** and **ft** as **f** as in **wrestle, often** and the other words given in this lesson.

LESSON 127: Introduce **ch** as a variant spelling of the **k** sound as shown in this group of words. Introduce **ps** as **s,** as in **psychic** and **psyche.**

LESSON 128: Introduce **y** as short **I** as in the words given in this lesson. Most of these words are of Greek origin.

With the completion of the final lesson, the pupil is now ready to start reading any suitable outside literature. Some pupils will require continued review of the alphabetic system in order to achieve real mastery.

Vocabulary expansion with multisyllabic words will be the major task in outside reading. This can start with fairly simple texts for beginning readers. The pupil should read as much as possible in order to practice his or her reading skills to the maximum. Of course, writing and spelling must accompany reading.

As for classroom reading, it is recommended that the teacher use a variety of poetry, fiction and nonfiction texts that will stimulate the students' appetite for the printed word. Libraries offer the young reader a tremendous variety of books on all subjects.

In introducing poetry to the students, choose poems with positive spiritual, patriotic, and narrative content. Children love these, and slow readers consider it quite an achievement to master these poems. Memorizing poetry and learning the words of the national anthem and other patriotic songs will help improve reading, comprehension, spelling, and speaking.

The **Bible** and **Bible** stories written for the young are particularly good sources of reading material. The stories themselves are fascinating, and the reader enters the vast realm of the spirit, expanding his horizon of philosophy and inner experience. Here the written word helps the student deal with the very meaning of existence, thereby demonstrating the importance of reading as a source of knowledge and a means of understanding what life is all about.

Another good way to get the child into the habit of reading is to introduce him or her to a popular adventure or detective series - such as the Hardy Boys and Nancy Drew. These books can create a voracious reading appetite and set a healthy pattern for life-long pleasure reading.

Tutors of older students will find excellent reading material in the **Reader's Digest.** A short article can be read aloud in one tutoring session with the student adding new vocabulary to the growing list in his notebook.

At this point it is important to get students into the habit of looking up in the dictionary the words they do not understand. That is the only way to increase one's reading and speaking vocabulary. Too many students retard their own intellectual growth by never bothering to look up the words they don't understand. The student must learn that there is no shortcut to vocabulary development, without which true literacy is impossible to attain.

Incidentally, never assume that a pupil knows the meaning of a word merely because he or she can read it. When in doubt, ask the pupil to define it.

Be on the constant search for good reading material for your students. Positive, uplifting, inspirational literature is eagerly read by young people seeking affirmation of life's value. Once the student realizes how much of real value can be found in the written word, reading will be an important part of that person's life.

Many teachers and tutors, in the course of using this instruction book will no doubt discover ways of improving it through practical use. The publisher would appreciate hearing from such teachers and tutors in order to incorporate such improvements in future editions.

ORDER OF LESSONS

153

ENGLISH ALPHABETIC SYSTEM

Sound   Common Spelling Forms

Vowels

short a   ă as in **cat**

short e   ĕ as in **met**; **ea** as in **bread**

short i   ĭ as in **sit**; **y** as in **myth, gym**

short o   ŏ as in **top**

short u   ŭ as in **cup**; **ou** as in **precious**

Long a   **a-e** as in **ate**; **ai** as in **wait**; **ay** as in **way**; **ei** as in **veil**; **eigh**

          as in **eight**; **a** as in **apron**; **ey** as in **they**

Long e   **ee** as in **tree**; **ea** as in **eat**; **ie** as in **field**; **e** as in **me**; **e-e** as in

          eve; **y** as in **happy, city**; **ei** as in **receive**

Long i   **i-e** as in **time**; **igh** as in **high**; **y** as in **try**; **ie** as in **lie**; **i** as in **item**

Long o   **o** as in **go**; **o-e** as in **home**; **oa** as in **boat**; **ow** as in **snow**; **oe** as in **toe**

Long u   **u-e** as in **use**; **ew** as in **new**; **ue** as in **true**; **iew** as in **view**

oo   **oo** as in **food**

oo   **oo** as in **good**; **oul** as in **could, should**

ou/ow   **ou** as in **out**; **ow** as in **cow**

oi/oy   **oi** as in **oil**; **oy** as in **boy**

a (ah)   **a** as in **car**; **father**

a   **a** as in **care, there, heir, fair**

a/au/   **a** as in **all**; **aw** as in **law**; **au** as in **cause**; **ough** as in **ought**; **augh** as in **taught**;

aw   **o** as in **loss**

er   **er** as in **germ**; **ir** as in **girl**; **ur** as in **fur**; **ear** as in **earn**; **or** as in **work**

o   **o** as in **born, core**

Consonants

b   **b** as in **bat, cab**

d   **d** as in **did**

f   **f** as in **fan**; **ph** as in **phone**; **gh** as in **rough, laugh**

g   **g** as in **get**; **gh** as in **ghetto**

h   **h** as in **house**; **wh** as in **who**

j   **j** as in **jam**; **g** as in **gem, angel, ginger**; **dge** as in **fudge**

(continued)

ENGLISH ALPHABETIC SYSTEM (con't)

Sound	Common Spelling Forms
k	k/ck as in **kick**; c as in **cat**; ch as in **chorus**; qu as kw (quit=kwit); x as ks (rex=wrecks)
l	l as in **lull**
m	m as in **mom**
n	n as in **nun**; kn as in **knee**
p	p as in **pep**
r	r as in **ran, car**; wr as in **wrap, write**
s	s as in **sell**; c as in **cell**; ps as in **psychic**
t	t as in **ten, net**
v	v as in **van, have**; f as in **of**
w	w as in **well**
y	y as in **yes**
z	z as in **zoo**; s as in **has**
th	th as in **the, with, father**
th	th as in **thin, think, truth**
ch	ch as in **chin, rich**; tch as in **catch**; tu as in **capture, picture**; ti as in **question**
sh	sh as in **she, wish**; ti as in **nation, patient**; s as in **sure**; ci as in **special, precious**
wh	wh as in **where, when**
zh	su as in **pleasure**; zu as in **azure**
n	ng as in **sing**; nk as in **sink**

Introducing Cursive

One of the most important tools of literacy that an individual must acquire is a good cursive handwriting. Cursive is a flowing form of handwriting in which all the letters of a word are joined. Manuscript, or print-script, which most children are taught in the first grade, is really a form of hand printing or lettering.

Most schools require children to learn cursive by the third grade. Unfortunately, many children fail to make a good transition from manuscript to cursive mainly because the third grade curriculum does not provide enough time for or supervision over handwriting development. The result is poor, often illegible handwriting.

But the simple truth is that most children can be taught cursive in the first grade, thereby eliminating the need for a difficult and chancy transition period in the third grade.

The virtue of teaching cursive in the first grade is that the teacher can spend more time supervising its correct acquisition. Also, the pupil begins developing an active tool of literacy which he or she will be using for the rest of one's life.

The most important task for the teacher in teaching cursive is to make sure that the pupil learns to hold the writing instrument correctly and form the letters correctly; that is, knowing where the letter starts and where it ends.

Cursive was developed to permit writers to obtain a fast, fluent, legible script with the minimum expenditure of energy. It takes time to develop a good cursive handwriting, and that is why it is wise to begin cursive instruction in the first grade.

Most children, as they learn the letter forms, begin writing cursive in a large awkward scrawl. This is quite natural because the child is being required to perform a manual physical task which requires considerable dexterity and precision. But in a few weeks or months that scrawl will evolve into a neat, legible script.

There are some youngsters - and adults - who experience great difficulty in learning to write. This is usually a physical problem that has nothing to do with intelligence. This condition is called dysgraphia and can only be overcome with a great deal of practice and perseverance. Dysgraphics usually find it equally hard to learn manuscript as well as cursive. Therefore, it makes sense to concentrate on cursive, since ultimately it is the more useful and required tool of literacy.

There are a number of good cursive instruction courses on the market that can be used in conjunction with ALPHA-PHONICS. Be sure to obtain one that shows the pupil how to form the letters in a correct series of steps. It is very important to teach the child to form the letters correctly the first time, for there is nothing more difficult than trying to break bad habits once they are acquired. Such future agony can be avoided by having the child do it right the first time.

For additional information about teaching cursive by this author, please refer to my book *How To Tutor*, which has a full section devoted to cursive.

CURSIVE
ALPHABET

Aa Bb Cc Dd Ee

Ff Gg Hh Ii Jj

Kk Ll Mm Nn

Oo Pp Qq Rr Ss

Tt Uu Vv Ww

Xx Yy Zz

PREREADING
ALPHABET
EXERCISES

A B C D E F G H I J K L M
N O P Q R S T U V W X Y Z
a b c d e f g h i j k l m
n o p q r s t u v w x y z

A B C   a b c
D E F   d e f
G H I   g h i
J K L   j k l
M N O   m n o
P Q R   p q r
S T U   s t u
   V W   v w
X Y Z   x y z

A	B	C		a	b	c
C	C	B		c	c	b
B	B	C		b	b	c
B	A	A		b	a	a
C	A	B		c	a	b
A	C	B		a	c	b
B	B	A		b	b	a
B	C	A		b	c	a
C	B	A		c	b	a
A	C	C		a	c	c
C	C	A		c	c	a
B	A	B		b	a	b
B	C	B		b	c	b
C	A	C		c	a	c
C	B	C		c	b	c

D	E	F	d	e	f
F	E	E	f	e	e
E	F	F	e	f	f
E	F	D	e	f	d
F	E	D	f	e	d
D	D	E	d	d	e
F	E	F	f	e	f
D	E	D	d	e	d
F	D	E	f	d	e
D	F	E	d	f	e
F	D	D	f	d	d
F	F	D	f	f	d
E	E	D	e	e	d
E	E	F	e	e	f
D	D	F	d	d	f
F	D	F	f	d	f

G	H	I		g	h	i
G	G	H		g	g	h
I	G	H		i	g	h
H	I	G		h	i	g
G	I	G		g	i	g
H	H	I		h	h	i
H	H	G		h	h	g
G	G	I		g	g	i
H	I	H		h	i	h
I	G	I		i	g	i
G	I	H		g	i	h
G	I	I		g	i	i
I	H	I		i	h	i
H	G	G		h	g	g
I	G	G		i	g	g

163

J	K	L		j	k	l
J	K	K		j	k	k
K	K	L		k	k	l
J	J	K		j	j	k
J	J	L		j	j	l
L	L	J		l	l	j
L	J	L		l	j	l
L	K	L		l	k	l
L	L	K		l	l	k
L	J	K		l	j	k
L	K	K		l	k	k
K	J	J		k	j	j
L	J	J		l	j	j
J	K	J		j	k	j
K	L	K		k	l	k

M	N	O	m	n	o
M	O	M	m	o	m
N	O	N	n	o	n
N	O	O	n	o	o
N	O	M	n	o	m
M	O	N	m	o	n
N	N	O	n	n	o
M	M	O	m	m	o
N	M	O	n	m	o
O	M	N	o	m	n
O	M	O	o	m	o
O	N	O	o	n	o
O	O	M	o	o	m
O	O	N	o	o	n
O	N	M	o	n	m

P	Q	R		p	q	r
P	Q	P		p	q	p
P	P	Q		p	p	q
R	R	Q		r	r	q
Q	Q	P		q	q	p
P	Q	Q		p	q	q
R	Q	Q		r	q	q
Q	R	Q		q	r	q
Q	P	Q		q	p	q
Q	Q	R		q	q	r
R	R	P		r	r	p
P	P	R		p	p	r
R	P	R		r	p	r
P	R	P		p	r	p
R	P	P		r	p	p

S	T	U		s	t	u
S	S	T		s	s	t
S	U	S		s	u	s
S	S	U		s	s	u
T	S	U		t	s	u
U	S	S		u	s	s
U	T	T		u	t	t
T	U	T		t	u	t
T	T	U		t	t	u
T	S	S		t	s	s
S	T	S		s	t	s
U	U	T		u	u	t
U	S	T		u	s	t
U	T	S		u	t	s
U	S	U		u	s	u

V	W	X	Y	Z		v	w	x	y	z
V	Y	W	X	V		v	y	w	x	v
Z	V	W	X	X		z	v	w	x	x
V	Z	Z	Y	W		v	z	z	y	w
W	W	Y	Z	X		w	w	y	z	x
X	X	Z	Z	Y		x	x	z	z	y
W	Y	W	Y	Z		w	y	w	y	z
Y	Y	Z	V	V		y	y	z	v	v
W	W	Z	Y	X		w	w	z	y	x
X	Y	Z	V	V		x	y	z	v	v
Z	Z	V	Y	X		z	z	v	y	x
Y	Z	Y	X	V		y	z	y	x	v
V	X	W	Y	Z		v	x	w	y	z
Z	X	Y	X	W		z	x	y	x	w
W	Z	X	Y	V		w	z	x	y	v

How To Tutor Workbooks
to accompany How To Tutor textbook: (no instruction in workbooks)

☐ **HTT Addition, Subtraction**..$24.95
89 pgs. 3 practice sheets for each lesson.

☐ **HTT Multiplication, Division, Fractions, Decimals**...................$24.95
110 pgs. 3 practice sheets for each lesson.

☐ **HTT Cursive Handwriting Practice Workbook**.........................$14.95
40 pgs. Exercises to build perfect handwriting.

☐ **Blumenfeld Oral Reading Assessment Test**...............................$24.95
How well does your child read? Find out easily
in privacy. Accurately determines grade level 2-12.
5 sets of Pre-Tests plus 5 sets of Post-Tests (For
after remediation).

☐ **Blumenfeld Oral Reading Test
Pronunciation Audio CD** $8.00
25 min. Clearly reproduces all 380 words of ea. test.

email: alphaphonics@
hotmail.com
ORDER FORM:
For shipping add $5.00 for first item. Add $3.00 for each extra book or CD. For UPS add
$6.00 to postal total. Canada: Add $5.00 to postal total (No UPS to Canada). Idaho
residents add 6% sales tax.

My payment for items checked above:

Shipping: _____

Sales Tax: _____

Total: _____

Name: _____

Street: _____

City: _____ *State:* _____ *ZIP:* _____

Phone No: (____) _____

Charge My: VISA Mastercard Discover AmExpress   Exp. Date ____
* (extra 3 digits found on signature side of card)

			*

*Make Checks
Payable to:*
**Paradigm Co.
3500 Mountain View Dr. Phone: (208) 322-4440 24 Hours-7 Days Ans. Machine
Boise, Idaho 83704**

☐ **NOW Alpha-Phonics book INCLUDES CD-ROM version inside the book
at NO extra charge; it's FREE**

☐ **Alpha-Phonics: A Primer for Beginning Readers**........................$34.95
Complete systematic, intensive phonics reading
program. All you need to teach anyone to read.
Now spiral bound for ease of use. Anyone can
teach with it. Now **includes $ 39.95 CD Rom free!**

☐ **CD Rom: Alpha-Phonics the Book on CD Rom if bought separately$39.95**
All the benefits of the Alpha-Phonics book plus wonders
of being on CD. You have to see it to believe it.
PC (Windows95-XP-Vista-Win. 7 & 8) No Apple (MAC).
You can download a free demonstration of the Alpha-Phonics
CDRom from our WEBsite to run on your own computer.
Go to our WEBsites: www.howtotutor.com or www.alpha-phonics
.com to get FREE first 4 lessons to preview.

☐ **Alpha-Phonics Audio CD-Rom set (2)***......................................$24.95
*All 128 lessons; all 44 speech sounds sounded out.
Make it easier to teach reading. CD's meant to aid,
not replace teacher.

☐ **How To Tutor the book: Teach 3-R's with one book**...............$29.95
Reading, cursive writing, arithmetic (gr. 1-6) 298pgs.

☐ **How To Tutor Pronunciation Audio CD***................................$8.00

☐ **How To Tutor Extra Large Type Student Lesson Book**.........$24.95
Accompanies HTT Book. Student's own big type
spiral bound lesson book. Makes it so easy for the
teacher and student! 177 pages.

☐ **Alpha-Phonics/HTT Phonics Reading Workbook***.................$19.95
Reinforces student learning. Practice sheets
supplement word and sentence writing. 47 pages.

☐ **Alpha-Phonics/HTT Little Companion Readers***...................$24.95
10 reader set, each with its own story. Vocabulary con-
trolled to coincide with the area of Alpha-Phonics
or How To Tutor in which you are teaching. You start with
Short A vowel Reader, then short E vowel Reader, and so on.

* These work with reading instructions in *How ToTutor or Alpha-Phonics*

ABOUT THE AUTHOR

SAMUEL L BLUMENFELD first became aware of the reading problem in 1961 when, as a book editor in New York, he was asked to join the National Advisory Council of the Reading Reform Foundation. The more Mr. Blumenfeld became aware of the reading instruction controversy, the more resolved he became to do something about it.

In 1972 he wrote THE NEW ILLITERATES in which he traced the history of reading instruction in America and diagnosed the causes of reading disability. He also traced the origin of the look-say method back to its inventor, Thomas H. Gallaudet, the celebrated teacher of the deaf. Since then Mr. Blumenfeld has taught in schools and tutored privately, developing his own system of intensive phonics.

ALPHA-PHONICS is the result of that thorough research and first-hand experience. "I wanted to create an effective, inexpensive and uncomplicated reading instruction program that could be used as widely as possible to help solve America's reading problem. With competent instruction, virtually anyone can be taught to read well."

Mr. Blumenfeld's other books include HOW TO START YOUR OWN PRIVATE SCHOOL -AND WHY YOU NEED ONE, HOW TO TUTOR, and IS PUBLIC EDUCATION NECESSARY? His writings on the literacy problem have appeared in *The Reading Informer, Education Digest, Vital Speeches, Boston Magazine, and Reason.*

Prior to authoring his books, Mr. Blumenfeld spent ten years in the New York publishing industry where he was First Reader of the Viking Press and Editor of the Universal Library at Grosset & Dunlap. He holds a Bachelor of Arts degree from the City College of New York.

$34.95   NOW ALPHA-PHONICS book includes CD ROM Version FREE!

This book can solve America's reading problem!

Letters to the author from parents:

I must write to express my wife's and my thanks for your excellent book. It has been so very valuable to us in teaching our 81/2 -year-old son, Eric, to read. . .

When I started on September 10th, Eric was almost totally restricted as a reader. Evidently he was one of those youngsters who refuse to attempt sight reading. I followed your book's instructions exactly. Would you believe that we went from Lesson 2 through Lesson 27 in two weeks? And by Thanksgiving we had drilled right through Lesson 117?

Even you wouldn't believe the results! It was as if we were witnessing a miracle!

Eric is now reading **Robinson Crusoe,** and is just loving it! He had been having headaches all through second grade and was losing weight. Since he started learning by your method, he hasn't been sick one day, and has gained weight rapidly to where he has a perfect physique.

Needless to say, we are grateful. Thank you so much for your excellent effort in helping countless parents, such as ourselves, in warding off the educational crippling of countless children.

> W.M.
> Westfield, New Jersey
> (now residing in Hendersonville,
> North Carolina)

My daughter is almost six years old and we are home educating her... I have tried a couple of reading programs, most of which were game type learning. None of these produced any results. I recently ordered **Alpha-Phonics** because I have heard Samuel Blumenfeld speak on several shows.

Dianna and I are just beginning lesson 5. After going over lessons three and four Dianna was so excited that she could read that she hugged my neck and told me she loved me. She said, "Oh mommy, my wish is coming true. You and Daddy are teaching me to read." What else can I say?

I love this systematic way of teaching reading because it produces immediate results and children, as well as adults, like to see progress.

By the way, *we only spend about five to ten minutes a day on this.* This is an excellent intensive, systematic phonics program.

> Thank you,
> C. M.

ISBN 978-0941995306

Paradigm Company, Boise, Idaho

ISBN 978-0-941995-30-6

9 780941 995306

Printed in Great Britain
by Amazon